The
HURRY-UP
Song

THE

Hurry-Up Song

A Memoir of Losing My Brother

CLIFFORD CHASE

HarperSanFrancisco
A Division of HarperCollins*Publishers*

Grateful acknowledgment is made for permission to quote from *The Healing Notebooks* by Kenny Fries © copyright 1990 by Kenny Fries. All rights reserved. Used by permission of Jed Mattes Inc., New York.

"On the Shoulder of the Road" originally appeared, in slightly different form, in *A Member of the Family: Gay Men Write About Their Families* and was excerpted in *The Bedford Reader* (Fifth Edition) and *Growing Up Gay*. "Leaving the Beach" first appeared in *Men on Men 5: Best New Gay Fiction*.

Some proper names, place names, and identifying details in this work have been changed to ensure the privacy of individuals.

FIRST EDITION

Book design by George Brown

Library of Congress Cataloging-in-Publication Data
Chase, Clifford.
The hurry-up song : a memoir of losing my brother / Clifford Chase. — 1st ed.
p. cm.
ISBN 0–06–251019–3 (cloth : alk. paper)
ISBN 0–06–251020–7 (pbk. : alk. paper)
1. Chase, Ken, 1952–1989—Health.   2. AIDS (Disease)—Patients—United States—Biography.   3. AIDS (Disease)—Patients—United States—Family relationships.   4. Gay men—United States—Biography.   5. Brothers.
I. Title.
RC607.A26C4783   1995   94-30209
305.38'9664'092—dc20   CIP
[B]

95 96 97 98 ❖ RRD/H 10 9 8 7 6 5 4 3 2 1

This edition is printed on acid-free paper that meets the American National Standards Z39.48 Standard.

Acknowledgments

For generous and inspired responses to this work at every stage of the writing, I'm indebted to Gabrielle Glancy, Catherine Kudlick, Wayne Koestenbaum, and my sister Carol Chase. For further advice and encouragement, thanks to my editor, Kevin Bentley, and to Bernard Cooper, Erin Hayes, Maggie Meehan, Ralph Sassone, George Russell, Robert Marshall, Noelle Hannon, and John Kureck. I'm also grateful to the late John Preston, since this book began as an essay for his anthology *A Member of the Family*. Thanks to the MacDowell Colony and the Corporation of Yaddo, where several chapters germinated, and to Diana Pearson at *Newsweek* for giving me time off work to complete this project. Finally, special thanks to David Rakoff, who spotted the book's title, and named the tune.

Contents

. . . And still I sit all day as if
choosing the right word could save your life.

KENNY FRIES
The Healing Notebooks

The
HURRY-UP
Song

On the Shoulder
of the Road

MY BROTHER KEN, who died of AIDS at thirty-seven, almost died in a car accident when he was three. My mother almost ran him over.

This was in Illinois, before I was born. So for me the accident takes place in a mythical prehistory that shapes everything to come. For me it's almost as if it takes place in the womb.

It was on a family trip. My father and Uncle Pete were in one car, with Ken and my oldest brother, Paul, in the wide backseat. Following in the next car was my mother, who was driving, and Aunt Helen and my two sisters. My father and uncle got involved in conversation and weren't watching the boys. Nor did the men notice that the doors were unlocked. Apparently Ken grew restless and decided to experiment with the door handle.

So, driving along a two-lane highway at sixty miles an hour, my mother sees my two brothers fly out of the car ahead of her. She swerved, my sisters say, to avoid the boys as they rolled on the pavement.

My brothers and the two cars all came to rest on the shoulder of the road. I imagine the cars were black or dark green, with tiny rounded windows, and there were light green wheat fields off to the right.

Miraculously, neither of my brothers was badly hurt: a chipped elbow for Paul, a broken leg for Ken. But this became one of the cautionary stories that ruled the family. After that, my father wouldn't pull an inch out of the driveway without making certain the car was secure. I remember we'd be all ready for a pleasant drive, and suddenly the air would be filled with tension. Urgently, sometimes angrily, my father would ask: "Did you lock your doors, boys?" To me, who came years after the near tragedy, his caution seemed ridiculous. And to this day, when any of us comes for a visit, my father continues the drill, even though obviously we're all adults, and no one is going to decide to just open the door when the car is hurtling down the highway.

KEN WAS IN A SENSE my only sibling. The others are much older and were all out of the house by the time I was seven. My sisters, born fourteen and sixteen years before me, are more like beloved aunts. And when I say "my brother," without using a name, I don't mean my oldest brother, Paul. I could only mean Ken.

My family moved a lot, so Ken and I spent a lot of time together, despite an age difference of six years. By the time we got to California, the two of us played and fought on surprisingly equal terms. Paul had been left in college in the last state, and my mother started working, so now it was just Ken and I at home. We moved across town only six months later, when my parents bought a house, so Ken and I had to change schools just as we were making friends; the two of us were thrown together again. I was nine and he was fifteen. We started playing a lot with a dozen or so hand puppets given to me by our Uncle John. First we told stories about them; then we started making props and clothing, and eventually, over the next couple of years, we created a whole world with them.

They were made of molded plastic and painted either blue or yellow. We called them muppets. The blue ones frowned and had bulbous green noses, and the yellow ones smiled with big red mouths. They came in pairs, stuffed in small corrugated boxes, and each of them had distinctive features depending on how it had been packed with its partner. To adults the muppets all looked the same, but Ken and I had no trouble telling them apart. For instance, one of the yellow ones had been smashed so flat in his box that his smile was completely gone, and he was doomed to live life in eternal profile. Ken named him Dead Codfish. He was a gangster.

We made the frowning blue ones female, which may have reflected my mother's temper, and perhaps an underlying sadness or fragility that we sensed in her. The yellow, smiling ones were always male, and they had high voices. One of them could play either Ken or me, or sometimes my father, in his amiable, accommodating mode. But my father could also be represented by a blue muppet. In our cartoons, if you were a yellow muppet and you got really angry, you'd turn into a blue muppet. But if you were a blue muppet you were always a blue muppet, and if you were angry you simply grew ten feet tall.

In fact, we made up a special word for the blue muppets to express their anger: *dih*. Pronounced like *dish* without the *sh*, it could be either a swear word or "blah-blah" for rage. Usually the blue muppets resorted to strings of "Dih" when reason failed them, pummeling the yellow ones into submission. I think my mother's moods made about as much sense to me when I was growing up: "Dih, dih"—die, die.

The muppets were my opportunity for revenge and conspiracy. Whenever Ken and I were in trouble, we could go into my room, shut the door, and reenact the scolding scene with my parents completely in the wrong. We drew cartoons, or set up scenes in their houses, and the parent muppets would rant and rave ridiculously.

Even my best friends at school never quite entered fully into the muppets' world: it was Ken's and mine. We used to say "Dih" to each other even as adults, which expressed both a particular kind of exasperation—that is, that we knew it was futile to be so mad—and the intimacy between us.

Ken made up countries for them, and each pair was a king and queen. They lived in suburban houses, open-topped corrugated boxes, and their furniture and clothes were mostly construction paper. I sat on the floor in my room for hours with the glue and scissors and Scotch tape. I wanted them to have everything on *Let's Make a Deal:* kitchen ranges, refrigerators, cars, boats, minks, sets of encyclopedias. My mother sewed them royal robes that tied around the neck, with terry-cloth fur trim. Ken and I cut up bits of paper and made money.

All the muppets were mine except one pair, which was Ken's. Harold and Victoria were rulers of the smallest but most powerful country, Heere. Harold owned the casino, where all the others lost their money. Victoria owned the Beauty Baths, which we set up every once in a while in the bathroom—some lounging in the sink, and others sitting to dry up on the plastic decorative shelves above the toilet, next to the fake fishbowl. This was the analog of the wig and beauty shop where my mother was bookkeeper, and about which she complained nightly at dinner. We soon discovered that the tap water actually helped chip the muppets' paint, which for them was a sign of aging. "So really they're Ugly Baths!" Ken cried.

(It was Harold and Victoria that I would search for most desperately in Ken's house in San Diego after he died. I couldn't find them, and so I took other childhood objects: Matchbox cars, his oldest stuffed animals, and two early hand puppets, Tiger and Ruff, a furry tiger and puppy whom I remembered but had never really played with. As it turned out, Harold and Victoria were still at my parents' house up in San Jose; I found them the following Christmas, staring up out of a box in the garage.)

For a time we took delight in making the muppets the most outlandish clothing and furniture, because Ken said they had a mental disease called *opposite-itis*. It meant they liked ugly things. I'd make a green checked bedspread and then put black and pink snowflake wrapping paper up on the walls. "How lovely!" Ken would exclaim, speaking in the high voice of the yellow muppet. "How elegant!" They had "bad taste," Ken said. Later they all got over it and had to redecorate.

COULD TWO straight brothers have constructed the same world? Or one straight and one queer? Somehow the answer is no, and lately I like to think of my time spent playing with the muppets as the height of a gay childhood.

As if to prove this, at school that world soon became suspect. It was said that Cliff *played with dolls*. For I made them clothes and furniture. "They're not dolls, they're *puppets*," I would reply. The muppets hardly resembled people, I reasoned, and their clothing and houses weren't at all realistic. Besides, I told myself, everything was made out of construction paper, and I didn't buy anything, the way a girl would buy Barbie clothes; I made everything myself.

Early in sixth grade I made the mistake of bringing a pair of muppets to math class one day, setting them up in the corner of my desk so I could look at their faces. Mr. Lang said I had to put them away, and then began asking pointed questions. *Do you play with them all the time? Do you sew them clothes? Do you make them dollhouses?* Like a doctor he nodded a short "uh-huh" to each answer, and then he turned in his gray suit back to the blackboard.

The year before, it had been Mr. Lang who wouldn't let me give a puppet show to his class. Perhaps my own teacher said something to me about his not approving. In any case, somehow

I knew Mr. Lang's refusal wasn't because he thought my show would disrupt his curriculum, but because of me.

It was also about then that the other kids began calling me names. My friend Chipper had moved away the year before, and my new friend, David Vickers, called me a fem all the time.

But at home in my room I still had my own, safe world if I wanted. Here there was nothing wrong with me. "The other kids play with G.I. Joe, don't they?" Ken would point out. "G.I. Joe is a doll."

Even as sixth grade went by and I began to move on from the muppets, it was always a world to return to—as Ken and I knelt on the floor beside the cardboard houses, and each took a puppet in hand. It might be a fight with my parents, or just plain boredom, that brought him into my room. But then we could draw a cartoon, or take the muppets and move them about in their open-roofed houses, which were growing dusty now, and act out a story.

So it was a refuge, but a betrayal was coming.

It was the summer before Ken went away to college. My mother, who worked full-time, was paying him to clean house for her, and baby-sit for me. Cruel opportunist, I defied Ken as much as possible, teasing him mercilessly when he was vacuuming or dusting. Like my parents, he had a terrible temper. It was easy even for me, six years younger, to get his goat. I would stand in the path of the vacuum cleaner and pull faces, or I'd follow him around while he was dusting and make farting noises. Sometimes I'd just lean in the doorway of the bathroom and stare at him until he turned from his cleaning and said, "Do you mind?"

David Vickers and I had set up the train table in the living room for the summer. In self-defense I had put the muppets aside and now played with trains every day, a more boyish activity. David and I had built plastic-girder bridges from the train table to the two steps into the sunken living room—and this was the cause of perhaps the worst fight I ever had with Ken.

It was hot, and the sunlight pressed against all the windows of the house. I had no doubt been teasing Ken all day, and now he wanted to vacuum the steps. I remember he came into my room and asked me to move the bridges.

"No," I said, fingering the curtains. "I don't feel like it."

He grabbed my arm, I began to squeal as shrilly as possible, and things went on from there. He managed to drag me out into the entryway above the living room, and he hit me a few times on the shoulder. Still I refused to help him. "Cleaning is your job," I said. By now he had pinned me to the cold tile floor and was kneeling over me, his face and arms red with fury. I struggled, and then came his worst blow:

"Stupid little faggot!"

He had never called me that before. Or if he had, somehow it had never hit me in quite the same way. We stared at each other a moment, and I think my face must have changed its shape. Maybe I screamed. What I felt, and could not find words for: *Not you, too.*

I wriggled loose and stumbled down the hall, a new and shameful grief flooding my eyes. It was one of the last times I would really cry as a child. Once I was in my room with the door closed behind me, that privacy did not seem enough either, and, as if to confirm the power of a future metaphor, I ran and shut myself in the closet.

Ken came into my room after me. Somehow I had known he would see the seriousness of the situation and not open the closet as well. He stood outside the sliding door, and I sat fingering the opaque plastic door handle, a round cap over a hole in the door that offered the only light. "Come on," he said. "I hardly touched you."

But I kept still. My head hurt with trying not to cry, and it was hot in there. Ken waited a moment longer. "What's the matter?" he asked.

As much as we fought, and as often as Ken hit me, he was sensitive and he knew when he had really hurt me. I think he was sorry now, but still I didn't speak. I couldn't have explained it anyway, and at that moment I just wanted to be left alone to cry.

"OK, be that way," he said, and I heard him go out.

THE FOLLOWING SPRING, it was a chance remark by Ken that made me understand that I was gay.

He came home one weekend from college with his girlfriend, Kathleen. This was Ken's first and only girlfriend. I don't remember my oldest brother, Paul, ever bringing anyone home, so such a visitor was entirely new to me. The air seemed charged with sexuality. My mother approached Kathleen gingerly, as if on tiptoe; my father teased her. On Saturday afternoon Kathleen and Ken sunbathed on lawn chairs in the backyard. I followed my mother out with the tray of iced tea, and as Kathleen walked barefoot to the patio in her yellow bikini, her browned hips and breasts flowing out, my mother exclaimed—as she always did during sexy scenes in movies on TV, imitating a huffy matron: "Well!"

I had been lonely since Ken went away to college, and I wanted to sunbathe myself now in his and Kathleen's brief presence. I wanted to know them, their private jokes, their world together. They called each other "Rabbit." They surfed. They smoked pot. They had a communal way of talking, Southern Californian and ironic, with certain phrases that seemed unusual and hip to me: "How odd," they'd croon. Or, "Mr. Meat says, 'Make a mess!' " I didn't know where the phrases came from or even what some of them meant.

Saturday night I went to the movies with them. Or maybe we went miniature golfing, I don't remember. By the end of the evening it was like I was drunk on their company. As we drove home, in the darkness of the backseat I grew more and more vivacious, trying to imitate them and their phrases as much as possible. Maybe I was really imitating Kathleen. Anyway, after seven months of junior-high constraint, I let go completely.

I like to think of that utterly fluid moment in seventh grade, before I quite knew the names of things, the proper boundaries between masculine and feminine, gay and straight—when my personality was so unformed and changeable that I could, with a little encouragement and excitement, let my guard down and emerge as a flaming queen of a child.

"Oh, how odd!" I cried, giggling. "Make a mess!"

I was scarcely aware of whether Ken and Kathleen were listening, so happy was I to be with my brother and his girlfriend, this wonderful alternative to my hate-filled life at school.

"Why are you acting so strange?" Ken asked as we turned onto our block. All the houses were dark.

I stopped and thought. I was so happy, I wasn't even offended by his question. "I don't know," I said. "I usually don't act this way. How am I acting?"

"Really femmy," was his reply. Maybe he was embarrassed in front of Kathleen. And yet I like to think there was a strangely nonjudgmental quality in his voice, as if he was simply describing a fact.

"Really?" I said.

"Yeah, femmy," agreed Kathleen genially. She didn't seem to care.

"Hmm," I said. I looked for a reason. "I am acting different. Maybe it's because of being with you two."

Then Ken said something very strange. I'll never forget it, though I don't remember his exact words, and it was only a joke. He said something like, "Maybe you're a *contact homosexual.*"

"What's that?" I asked.

And he explained that it was someone who was homosexual only in contact with certain people, or in certain situations. It was a phrase he and Kathleen had learned in psychology.

Shame began to ring in my head like a bell. We had pulled up in the drive a few minutes ago, and now we got out of the car. As I followed them up the dark walk to the house, in the California night air, I was beginning to put it together—what *homosexual* was, what *fag* was, what I was. The revelation was a physical sensation: I think my hair was standing on end. Inside, I said good night to my parents, who were getting ready for bed. Ken and Kathleen went to their rooms—they had to sleep separately—and I went to my own room quickly, as if holding my discovery close to my breast. I closed the door, looked up the *H* word in the *Encyclopaedia Britannica*, and confirmed that I really was what the other boys at school said I was.

KEN CAME OUT to me when I was twenty-one. He had been living with Kathleen nearly six years when he started seeing men. He had moved with her to the East Coast, where she was getting her Ph.D., but he couldn't find work in Vermont and had to move to Boston. Now, a year and a half later, they had broken up and he had just moved back to California. He was staying with my parents while he looked for a job, and so now it was I who came home from college to visit one weekend.

Saturday night we went to a ferny, brightly lit bar in the next town where you could play backgammon. We sat down and had beers.

I didn't know Ken had something to tell me. His initial strategy was to remark how other men in the bar were cute. I was so far from letting myself look at men that I had no idea what he was talking about. I remember at one point a stocky blond guy came in the door, at the far end of the room. Ken pointed discreetly. "Oh, there's a cute one," he said.

I turned. "Uh-huh," I said vaguely, guardedly.

I must have been frowning.

"Do you think it's strange for me to say that?" Ken asked.

"I don't know. I guess you're scoping out the competition, huh?" I meant his competition for the women in the bar. I genuinely thought this was some sort of "swinging singles" technique.

Ken did one of his joking double takes, a fidgety gesture he had. He was always very nervous, his hands shaky, and his eyes darting in the manner of everyone in the family, to your face and shyly away again. He had ruddy skin and a high forehead that furrowed easily. "Not exactly," he said. Then he just blurted it out: "I'm trying to tell you that I'm gay."

I almost think I had the same feeling of fear as that night when I was thirteen, when Ken made that chance remark—only now the feeling was more like elation. "Really?" I said. I saw him fidgeting with his beer, waiting for my reaction. It was as much to put him at ease as to satisfy any desire to talk about these things that I told him about myself too. "I've had those feelings," I said, faltering. Then I was a little more honest: "Actually I've had them a lot."

Ken did another one of his false double takes. But he was happy now.

We talked first about our mutual surprise. "I guess I always thought you were basically straight," Ken said.

"No . . . I thought that about you, too." And I have a particular image in my mind of Ken as a straight man, which was perhaps my model for any straight man: Ken washing his red Ford Falcon in the driveway. His teenager's manly persona was, in fact, part of my own ideal self-image, nurtured throughout high school—the kind of guy who fixes things, who swears, who smartly ruffles the newspaper before he begins to read. Somehow all that time Ken and I each believed in this "basically straight" guy, and we each fooled ourselves with him.

So it was that we began to compare notes. I had had no experience and was still too scared to be planning any, so I had little to tell. I did manage to say I had felt this way since I was five. Ken countered that he had had no sexuality at all until after high school. In the back of my mind, I attributed this to the family's moving constantly, which meant that Ken went to three elementary schools, two junior highs, and three high schools. It seemed logical that he might protect himself by feeling nothing sexually. But I wonder now just how much to believe him, or just what he really meant. Anyway, he explained that it was in graduate school in San Diego (the city where he would later settle, and where he would die) that he started looking at men: "On the beach, when I used to go surfing," he said. "The other guys."

This probably seemed a little too real to me at that moment: sitting on the beach; surfers in wet bathing suits; looking at them . . . But the story continued.

Back east, he and Kathleen had to live apart, and they began to fight. In Boston Ken started seeing a guy from work on the side. Within a few months Kathleen figured out something was up. Ken had never even hinted to her anything about being attracted to men, so she assumed he was seeing another woman. There was the expected confrontation. "I told her, 'No, I'm seeing a man,'" Ken explained, smiling angrily now, seeming to take a certain pleasure in that exchange—the kind of scene where you're holding all the cards, and you lay them all on the table at once.

"So what happened?" I asked.

There were more fights, he said, and he and Kathleen stopped speaking altogether for a while. Then Kathleen started seeing someone else, in Burlington, and she and Ken decided finally to break up.

There was a pause. Ken was upset, and I imagine him frowning and staring down at the table, the same frown he'd had since childhood.

Then began the most curious part of the conversation.

"Why do you think you're gay?" I asked.

Ken waited a minute and said, "I think it was because of the accident." He meant when he was three.

I knit my brow. "How is that related?"

Then he said: "I could have died, you know . . . I think after that, Mom clung to me too much."

Domineering mother, distant father: I think they were even in the *Encyclopaedia Britannica*. But even then I didn't put much stock in what Ken was saying, or maybe I was just jealous of the idea of his being so close to my mother—so I tried to make a joke of it all. "Well," I said, "I wasn't in any accident. So how does that explain me?"

BUT NOW I, too, want to make connections to that accident, as a way of creating some kind of order from my brother's life. My mind skips between past and present, searching. I want to see a senseless event, Ken's illness, as part of some larger pattern.

For instance: it was always said that when Ken was three, after he returned from the hospital, he never complained about the cast on his leg. Similarly, my mother says, he never complained as she and my father cared for him in the last months of his life.

But more important: it was a car accident that marked the onset of my brother's final illness. Suffering from dementia, he ran his car off the road one day and was found wandering like a three-year-old along the banks of the freeway. Paramedics took him to the hospital, but this time there was no miracle. His moments of lucidity were less and less frequent, he was in great pain, and he died, more quickly than expected, just two months later. So I lost him by the side of the road. I wasn't present at his first accident, which was before I was born, nor at his last one, which took place three thousand miles away, and I was on my way to visit him when he died.

Hope

S I WALKED with my mother from the airport gate, she told me that Ken couldn't make it this weekend after all. "He has the flu," she said. "I told him not to worry about it." The family was gathering in San Jose for my parents' fiftieth wedding anniversary. "Of course he still has to pay for the ticket," she went on. This was perhaps her way of wondering if this might be serious. One did not lightly throw away either money or airline tickets.

"That's a drag," I murmured, suddenly feeling like a net was tightening around me. At the time I was the only one in the family who knew that Ken was HIV-positive. My parents didn't even know that he was gay, or that I was either.

"So, what exactly did he say was the matter?" I asked. We had reached the luggage carousel, which with a groan began to turn like a great roulette wheel.

"Oh, he said it's just something hanging on." She patted her hair nervously. Whether she was concerned, or simply distracted, I couldn't tell.

I looked past her head out the plate-glass windows. The small airport was surrounded by fields, and at the edge of the parking lot I could just see the line of eucalyptus and willows, following a creek. Over the summer Ken had begun to have frequent health problems: fatigue, weekly rashes, a string of colds that each took weeks to go away. One doctor, as much as a year before, had mentioned ARC, but Ken just switched doctors. "Why scare me like that?" he had said.

My mother motioned to the center of the carousel, which had begun to spit suitcases onto the wheel. "He thought he'd better stay in bed," she mused.

"Sounds like it," I replied, nodding too vigorously. Anyone can get the flu, I thought.

Abruptly my mother turned, craning her head. "Where *is* Dad?" She blew out air in anger, and I began to feel even more tense. "I told him in front of *Baggage*." She went hurriedly to the window and then back again, shaking her head, setting her lips.

Ken and I would simply have made a joke of it all, lapsing into childhood language as soon as we were alone. "I'm home," the happy yellow muppet would sing. "Dih!" the blue one would yell. "Dih, dih!"

I saw the weekend unfolding before me then, without him. I would have to face them alone.

LEAVING THE AIRPORT, my father's old green car had trouble accelerating up the highway ramp. Going much too slowly, my father merged into traffic, not even turning his silver head, implacable as a tank. A car honked, and my foot went down to an imaginary brake.

My mother looked resolutely out the window. I knew this meant: "I don't argue with him."

I leaned forward. "So, are you excited about your anniversary?"

My mother did not turn her head. She seemed slumped on one side. "Oh, yes," she replied.

My father didn't hear the question, or he assumed I was talking only to my mother.

"I almost got put in first class," I said cheerfully. I wanted to entertain. As always upon first arriving, I felt childish and excited, brimming with stories of my life. If only I could think of what stories would interest them. "They had overbooked."

"That happened on our trip to Tahiti," my mother said, and the tale began.

As she spoke, I watched the tops of their two gray heads, just visible above the high headrests. I had ridden, alone, in the back of this car with them since seventh grade, when Ken went away to college.

"I bet you're glad to be out of that filthy city," my father said, all of a sudden. We flew along the highway above countless identical houses.

"Yeah," I said, trying to be agreeable. "New York's a mess."

"Too many niggers," my father said.

I cleared my throat.

Soon we reached the old neighborhood. Although we moved a lot when I was little, this had been our home since

I was ten. Treeless street, low ranch-style houses packed closely, camper shells in the driveways. My father aimed the remote control like a gun at our garage door, and we glided in next to my mother's Dodge.

There was just enough room to open the car doors on one side. My father had to slide across the front seat to my mother's door. I stood behind her as she made way for him.

"I still expect to see Sam," I said. Sam had to be put to sleep two years before.

"Yes," my mother agreed, finding her house keys. She had cried when she took him to the vet that last time.

My father unlocked the trunk for me. "Sam was a good dog," he said with finality. He handed me my suitcase.

I OPENED my bag on my old dresser. There were two beds in here now, and this was the room Ken and I always shared on visits home. I looked at the extra empty bed, the smooth blue spread.

"Knock, knock," said my mother. She stood in the doorway in her running shoes.

"Your father's taking a nap," she whispered, though he could not possibly hear her, "and I'm going for a walk."

I said I'd go with her. I had had an idea of this being a special weekend of getting to know my parents. Busily I changed into tennis shoes.

Outside, the sun went in and out of very clear-edged clouds. It was just the beginning of the rainy season, almost Halloween. I was tired. The night before, in New York, I had gone out dancing late with friends and ended up necking with a boy I met, upstairs on a couch overlooking the dance floor. I was surprised at myself. I hadn't even gone out on a date with anyone in almost two years. Something about its being my last chance before going to California, and here I was, 2 A.M., at a club called The World. . . . "Who are we?" I said to the boy, my hand on his cheek. "The people you see necking as you walk by?"

My mother and I crossed to my old school and walked down the gravel pathway, only recently made but already full of weeds, the stones overflowing their boundaries. Small, newly planted trees leaned this way and that, some fallen over entirely.

"Vandals," my mother complained.

But as we passed beyond the old backstop I could see the mountains above the houses, their peaks shrouded, rags of clouds sitting in the treed ridges. As a teenager, I had often come by myself to this field and looked hard at these mountains, trying to take in their peacefulness, to attain to them. Once they had actually calmed me. It was at the end of a bad flu. I had gone outside for the first time in a week or more, on a bright, clear day, and standing in the new wind beheld the mountains, blue with trees, perfectly clear. Suddenly I saw it: I was well now.

". . . he's driving me crazy," my mother was saying. She looked behind, in the direction of the house. "He took my car to that darned idiot at the gas station again. I *told* him to take it to the dealership instead. Well, it hasn't worked right ever since."

She was walking slowly and staring down at the weedy, pebbly ground. This was a continuation of a conversation my mother and I had had since I could remember. It wasn't that I often heard my parents fighting when I was growing up. Mostly I heard this.

"Anytime you go around a corner, it stalls," my mother was saying.

"Couldn't you take it to the garage yourself?" I asked, adopting my old helpful tone. But my head had already begun to tingle with frustration. Only an hour into my visit, and I was totally hooked in. "You could tell Dad you'll get the car fixed yourself."

She put on her child's face, imitating my father. "*Whatcha wanna do that for? Wuh, wuh, wuh.*"

"I FEEL like a butterfly!" Janet said, throwing her arms around me. I had come to meet her at the gate, and now I walked once again down the same tiled hallway to Baggage. "I've been through so much this past year," Janet explained. "But now it's like I've come out of my cocoon!" She turned to me confidentially. "Did Mom come to the airport too?"

I nodded. "She's in the car."

This was, in fact, the first time Janet had been home in almost fifteen years. She and my mother had argued one Christmas Eve, over the quality of the soft water in the house, and Janet had to go stay in a motel. After that she went to South America or the Bahamas for Christmas.

But now that Ken couldn't come, it was just Janet and I. Though the family was big—five children—the anniversary celebration would be small. My sister Carol was in France this year and couldn't get away. And Janet's coming meant my oldest brother, Paul, and his wife certainly would not, since Paul and Janet had not spoken in eight or ten years. It had to do with Janet feeling let down during some crisis.

"I think it will be all right for me to stay at the house," Janet was saying. She looked even more tiny than usual, her hair pulled back tightly. She is fourteen years older than me and we did not grow up together, but we had taken an interest in each other one year when we both lived in New York. Of all the members of the family, she looks the most like me. "I have my coping mechanisms built up," she said. "I didn't use to have that. And it's only one weekend, so I don't even have to take a shower if I don't want to. I won't have to use that awful water."

I cleared my throat. "Good," I said uncertainly, trying to ignore her last remark.

Here we were again by the circling carousels. But Janet had checked no luggage. This was only a meeting place. I nodded to the double glass doors.

Outside it was very, very bright. I couldn't see my parents' car. We waited, scanning the lot.

"I'm really glad you're here," Janet said to me, lifting her bright red carry-on bag and setting it down again. "We can keep each other sane."

Shortly my parents drove up, looking like two cut-outs in glasses sitting in the front seat. My mother got out of the car first. I watched her and my sister hug awkwardly, briefly. They were nearly the same size, my mother just a little taller.

I couldn't help but hope that this was an important reconciliation scene. "Is that everything?" my mother asked, pointing to Janet's one small bag.

She nodded with exaggerated brightness. "It's only two days, Mom."

KEN CALLED around lunchtime. Everyone got on the phone. He was coughing a lot.

"Oh, it's this damn flu," he said. "I caught it from this guy at work. I told him to stay away from me."

My mother chuckled. Tonight's plans for the anniversary celebration were discussed. Janet gave Ken a recipe for lemon tea. I lay in my father's dark study on the floor, holding on to the extension and looking up at the ceiling and the plaid drapes.

"Well, OK, Hon," my mother said to Ken at last. "Go take a nap."

"Yes," I said.

"Yes," said my father. "Rest."

"That's the main thing," Janet said.

After lunch I shut myself in my parents' room and called Ken back. I sat down on the floor next to my parents' bed, the place of all my secret phone conversations of high school.

"So, how are you doing?" I asked again.

He groaned. "Dih, dih, my throat hurts." I chuckled. "My doctor said it looks like a virus."

So it wasn't pneumonia, and certainly not *the* pneumonia. "I guess you just need to take it easy," I suggested. "Are you taking good care of yourself?"

"Yeah." He spoke defensively. Then: "Actually, I'm pretty worried."

"Well, sure," I said automatically. I had this uncanny way

then of being able to acknowledge that he had every reason to worry, that it was only natural to worry, all the while reassuring myself that in reality he had nothing to worry about. I preferred to think his illness was all in his head.

"They did some more tests this week," he said. "My doctor says I need to make a decision now about whether to go on AZT."

I blinked. This was something Ken had never mentioned before.

"My T-cell count is very low. The doctor was really scaring me. He said, 'With that T-cell count, you *will* get sick.'"

I stood up, stretching the phone cord, looking into the mirror above my mother's dresser. I saw myself there, standing alone in my parents' bedroom. The window behind my head was bright, and it was hard to see my face. The receiver seemed attached to my cheek like a big, white fishhook.

"God," I murmured. "Really." I tried to recover my equanimity, my calm, sympathetic tone.

Ken said he didn't know what to do, whether to risk the side effects of the drug. "I don't want that poison in my system," he cried, suddenly sounding like a cranky old man.

With AZT, I said to myself, it might be a long, long time before he got sick; and perhaps then they would find another drug, and then another still. . . . "On the other hand," I said hopefully, perhaps too urgently, "maybe it's better to try it and deal with the side effects while you're still healthy."

He grunted that that might be true, and then there was a pause. I changed the subject. "Mom and Dad are driving me crazy already." I wanted him to be a big brother again, to reassure me. "I'm really dreading this dinner tonight."

He cleared his throat loudly. "Did you go out and get the VCR yet?"

We had originally planned that all five of us would get together and buy them one, since Mom and Dad liked old movies and it seemed like a VCR was something they might use. But somehow we couldn't connect and ended up not buying the gift. "No," I said. "I thought we decided not to, right?"

"I forgot . . ."

There was something disturbing about that, as if maybe he had been too preoccupied lately to remember such things. Was he that sick?

I told him that Janet and I had gone in together on a present, which I bought last week in New York. But now Ken had to buy them something. "Well, I have a good excuse," he said, meaning he was home with the flu.

"So you're seeing the doctor Monday?" I asked.

"Yes," he said with irritation. There was a noise. He was fiddling with something, perhaps in the kitchen. I shouldn't have brought it up again.

"Well, I really wish you were here. Now I don't know when I'll see you."

I heard the noise stop. "You're not coming home for Christmas?" There was a sudden urgency to his voice, and it frightened me.

"I hadn't intended to," I said. "I thought this would be my trip to California for the year." I picked up my mother's little daily prayer booklet from her dresser, observed the picture of Palestine on the cover. I set it down again. "Yes, well, maybe I could."

"I really wish you would," Ken repeated.

I sighed, equivocated again—as if that were also equivocating with his impending illness, a way of evading or confusing fate. Some part of me feared keenly that we had already entered into a region where final requests were being made.

WE STOOD around the table looking at the small, brown package. It had just arrived from my brother Paul and his wife. My father came back from the kitchen with a pair of scissors and sat down. Meticulously he undid the wrapping, first slitting the tape on all four sides. He had been an engineer before his retirement ten years ago.

"Hurry up!" I said. "It's a present."

My father only laughed, carefully pulling open the box to reveal a second, blue-wrapped rectangle. In turn he unwrapped this box, carefully folding the fancy paper so it could be reused. He opened the box.

It was a videotape.

My mother looked puzzled.

" 'Paul, Cynthia, and the kids,' " my father read out from the label. "Must be a home movie."

I glanced at Janet and back to my mother.

"We were thinking of getting you a VCR," I confessed. "But then we didn't." Ken, I remembered, was supposed to tell Paul about our change in plans. I giggled nervously. "I guess Paul didn't know."

The truth was, I took a certain evil pleasure in the incident. For years I had barely had any contact with Paul, who had more or less joined his wife's family and never came home for the holidays. And because I was more in touch with Janet, I had tended to take her side in their long-standing dispute. I was also annoyed that he, who made much more money than any of us, appeared to consider a single home video as his contribution toward an expensive anniversary present. And to me the tape of his family seemed to say, "I'm married and I have two children. (I'm not gay. I'm not abnormal in any way. I'm not sick. . . .) That's the best gift I could ever offer Mom and Dad."

The black plastic rectangle sat forlornly on the table, no player in sight.

My mother picked it up. "Oh, well. We can go play it on the Johnsons' next door." I couldn't tell if she was disappointed or not, whether she was hurt to learn of our abortive plans—the gift promised, then taken away.

HIGH VIOLIN scales labored from my mother's study, and the tap-tap of a hurried metronome. The sun grew yellow in the frosted window of the hall, and it was Halloween. The notes stopped, and soon my mother emerged to place a single bowl of candy on the chest by the front door, for the little ones who might come early.

"After that, we'll be out to dinner," she said. "So I didn't bother buying any more candy." I imagined the costumed children of the block, passing our dark and empty house all night. "They'll get plenty of candy without us," my mother added.

"Aw," I cooed, but I was glad not to have to listen to the doorbell all night. I put my book down and followed her back into her study, where her violin lay in its open case. She'd always played in amateur orchestras, wherever we lived.

"There just aren't that many kids left anyway," my mother went on. The school around the corner had recently been closed and might be turned into a senior center, she explained, wiping her bow with a light blue cloth. "Besides, it's not like it used to be, where you trusted everyone," she said. I imagined our old neighborhood in Connecticut, mythical to me because I had grown up here instead. "There's always some crazy idiot. Trick-or-treating has gotten too dangerous."

An hour later, driving to the restaurant, we saw them, in witch's hats with plastic pumpkin baskets, going from house to house. Meanwhile in New York, I thought, my haircutter Tim would be out in black mantilla and lace, towering spike heels— "The Seven-Foot Widow," he called himself—and he and the costume parade would snake through the Village, drag queens with pom-poms and feather fans stopping the trucks and cabs on Seventh Avenue. . . .

"I don't see why we have to go out to dinner," said my father with his peculiar blend of petulance and complacency. We had just pulled onto the freeway. "Mom's cooking is better." Before us, rows of red taillights made their way to the other side of the city.

"It's a celebration," Janet tried.

My mother looked out the window at the dark, and I settled back into the cave of the backseat. One dinner out was all we could convince my parents to do for their anniversary. No cake, no friends, no party. Just a family dinner, and now it was just the four of us.

I was disappointed in them. "Don't you want a big party?" I had asked, months before. But they didn't. I wondered if they had anyone to invite anyway.

"There'll be a cake at Mariners," my mother said, referring to their church couples group. "I don't see any point in making a big fuss."

THE RESTAURANT was a suburban town's attempt at sophistication, serving dishes like blackened catfish with mango chutney. Janet and I had found the place in a guide, since all my parents could suggest was the Sizzler. We ordered, and my father made jokes about the menu with the waitress, who didn't laugh.

My father passed me the bread. "Want some potato pancakes?"

I had to laugh. This was his particular brand of humor. "No, I'll have brussels sprouts with whipped cream." I passed the bread to my mother.

She lifted the linen napkin to reveal two small, tan loaves. "Oh, baby anteaters!" she said, taking one.

This kind of levity, frequent when I was growing up, rarely lasted long now. Janet began asking my parents lots of questions. She was in high, fragile spirits, and she drank a lot. "I'm playing journalist," she exclaimed, pretending to hold a microphone. Over the course of the meal, my parents told how they met, where they got married, where they first lived in Illinois. These were all old stories, canned-sounding, and nothing seemed to explain anything about them or why they had been married all these years. Apparently the occasion of the anniversary hadn't sparked any new insights. I couldn't seem to grasp the conversation's thread, and as usual at family gatherings since what seemed like the beginning of time, I grew sullen and didn't feel like talking.

Looking across the bright, half-empty restaurant, I wished Ken were there. Even if he didn't liven up the conversation, at least I would have someone to talk to when we got home. "I'm gay, and so is Ken," I imagined saying, picturing the kind of defiant and utterly triumphant moment with my parents that periodically I dreamed about.

After dessert, it was time to open presents. Since Janet and I were the only siblings there, and since the two of us had pooled resources, there was only one present. My mother untied the single ribbon and lifted the lid of the box. Here was the big moment, and it happened rather quickly.

"Oh," she said indifferently, folding aside the top layer of tissue paper.

We had bought them monogrammed towels. Dark pink for my mother, with white letters, and white for my father, with dark pink letters.

"Huh," said my father.

I had to admit to myself then that it was a ridiculous gift. "I don't know," I said, taking a sip of wine. "I just thought they were really beautiful." I reassured myself that Janet and I were also giving them this nice dinner out. Firstlings of the flock as well as fruit of the ground.

"Oh, yes," my mother agreed. She left the towels neatly folded in the box, looking down at them as if they were a baby that couldn't be disturbed. (The following day, she would wash them together, and my father's white towels would turn pink.)

"Very nice," my father put in politely. They put the box down and looked at us. They sat side by side, as inscrutable as two cats. They both wore gold-framed glasses, their eyes small and pale blue behind the reflections. I noticed again how gray they both had become.

"So, what's it like—fifty years?" Janet asked.

My parents shrugged.

2.

There was to be no catharsis or showdown that weekend. There was no scene between my mother and father, or between my sister and my mother, or between me and either of my parents. I didn't come out to them; I didn't tell them about Ken, or the state of his health. The next morning Janet flew off, neither fully reconciled to my mother nor more at odds with her than she had been before. In the afternoon my mother called Ken, and he said he was getting better. He would go to work tomorrow.

I wolfed my dinner, sat toying with my fork as my parents continued eating in silence. An old unease was stealing over me, as familiar and pervasive as the smell of this house. I excused myself, wandered down the hall to my room, and lay down, my hand on my chest. Enveloped in secrets and anticlimax, I was wobbling off center, and how could I right myself? The loose-weave curtains dangled near my head. I lifted one corner, peered out at the big star of the streetlight, let the curtain drop again.

I still had a few days left in California. Tomorrow I was headed to Berkeley to see my friend Cathy, and we were going camping. Later in the week I was going to visit my old friend Mike in Santa Cruz. But tonight I didn't know what to do with myself.

I went back out to the family room: the TV on, my father in his reclining chair, and my mother in her place in the corner of the brown couch, knitting silently, just like it always was. For six years, in junior high and high school, after Ken went away to college, it was just me and them.

My father held out a lemon drop. "Want one?" His mouth was full of them.

I sat down. "Sure." I took the lemon drop from him. He held the glass jar of candy on his lap and watched the screen.

My mother, too, stared over her knitting at the TV. I dropped the candy in my mouth, rolling my tongue over its rough, sugary surface. In the background, the dishwasher hummed. The TV was blaring so that my mother could hear, and I felt a kind of paralysis coming on, and then panic, adrenaline chasing the sleeping drug.

How could I escape?

The second half of *Murder, She Wrote* came on, and I ran into my room to get my address book. I had to find someone to see tonight. I had to get out of the house!

The only friend I had left in town was Pat Heaney. I knew him from church, and he had been one of three boys who more or less replaced my brother's companionship when he went away to college. Now I spoke to Pat maybe once every six months. He had had a breakdown of some kind in his freshman year of college, and after that it was drugs, a series of telephone-sales jobs, abortive stints in school. Pat was painfully skinny, and he had suffered perhaps the worst acne of anyone I'd ever known. He seemed trapped in San Jose. Eventually he had settled down to work for his father's hardware store, but last year when Pat told his family he was gay, his father fired him. Mr. Heaney said he had to protect his employees from catching AIDS.

Still, the last time I talked to him, Pat had joined AA, started excercising, and was planning to go back to school again. I reassured myself now that things were looking up for Pat, and it would be nice to see him tonight if he was free. It would be good to connect with an old friend.

And as in high school, when I was alone in the house with my parents, it seemed that my absolute survival depended on calling him. So, gasping like a fish, I dialed.

He answered after just one ring. His voice sounded a little odd, but I was so happy to reach him. Thank God he was home, I said. Did he want to go out for coffee with me? My parents were driving me nuts.

There was only the slightest pause. "I'm really glad you called," Pat said evenly. "Because today is probably the worst day of my entire life."

PAT DIDN'T have a car, which in San Jose is one step away from being homeless, so I agreed to come pick him up. I could hardly back out now. My only comfort was putting on my new, very expensive raincoat, which I had been saving for some evening out in California.

Pat had lost his latest job the day before, and he was about to be thrown out of his apartment. Some of his stuff was in boxes, some of it strewn around the living room. "I've been really dysfunctional for months," he explained. He wandered about, kicking through his things. "Just a minute," he said distractedly.

His face was broken out again, and his shoulders were narrow in an old gray sweater that was much too big for him. He had already lost most of his pale hair, and he had a small, round potbelly. A cigarette quivered in his mouth, unlit. "Someone's helping me move tomorrow," he said, gesturing toward the mess. He started going through a drawer, which lay on the carpet out of its dresser. "Now, where are they?" he muttered.

I realized he meant his house keys. "Huh," I murmured, as if a reply were necessary. I stood in the middle of the living room, clutching my raincoat. I folded it into a soft, brown-green package. "You'll find them," I said.

The keys turned up in a pair of pants that lay in a pile on the carpet. He put them in his pocket, patting them, his too-big jeans hanging loosely off his hips. "OK," he said. He turned to me abruptly. "It's so good to see you!" he cried, and he reached out and hugged me very tightly.

I remembered then how Pat used to hug me when we were teenagers, how once after I had invited him to Talent Night at my high school, as we sat waiting out front for my mother to pick us up, he put his arm over my shoulder. He pretended it was a joke. "We're fags, we're fags," he sang, squeezing me. But the next morning the story was all over school.

In fact, I often dreamed about Pat Heaney. Even now, I was still in the closet at work, not to mention with my family. And only a little more than two years earlier, I still had a girlfriend. So lately Pat appeared to me in various scenarios of embarrassment; somehow he had come to embody everything I found scary about being gay. He was, to use an expression Pat himself once invented, my "personal nightmare"—the figure I was afraid I would become. Often the dream would entail trying to avoid him, but then he would pop up again later, at an important party perhaps—pocked, eccentric, entreating . . .

We went to the door. "Oh," he said, stopping at a little table. The phone machine was blinking. "Maybe that's my money." He pressed a button and the tape rewound, making squiggling noises before it began to play.

It was his mother, saying she could lend him only fifty. "I'm sorry, that's all I can do. . . . I guess you'll have to try Jack."

Pat laughed with theatrical bitterness, shutting off the machine. Jack was what he and his mother called his father, ever since the divorce. "We try to avoid Jack at all costs," Pat said. He shook himself slightly. "Anyway . . . "

He turned to me and tried to smile, motioning to the door. "Precipice Pursuit!" he cried, recalling the alternative for Cliff Chase he had once so cleverly devised.

WE SAT in the only café in San Jose, on blue plastic chairs overlooking a badly stocked bookshop. Pat was smoking now, holding his cigarette to one side with the forced casualness of Barbara Stanwyck. "I haven't paid my rent in four months," he said a little wildly. "I have to be out tomorrow unless I can come up with five hundred." He pushed back the few remaining hairs above his forehead. "But I'm sure it will all work out."

I asked him if he had any place to stay, and he said his friend Larry from the Program would put him up. "Larry's great," he said, with a curious flatness.

He stubbed out his cigarette, and I looked at the pictures on the wall a moment, spirals and geometric shapes, the efforts of the local college students.

"So this weekend was weird," I said distractedly, falling back on our teenage ways of talking about our parents. "The celebration was kind of awful. . . . And it turned out Ken couldn't make it."

Pat tried to look interested, and he managed a concerned, kind expression.

"Flu," I said. I began picking at my Styrofoam cup. "But he's HIV-positive, you know." I didn't mention the news about his T-cell count.

Pat only grunted, so I changed the subject. I was happy to, anyway. "So, what else is happening with you?" I asked, as if this were any normal day for him, a pleasant evening for two old friends to catch up.

Pat explained he had been going out with a nurse and former prison guard who had suffered several heart attacks even though he was only thirty-two. Pat met him at an AA meeting at the gay church across the street from his apartment. First he was on crutches, next in a wheelchair, and then a few months ago he disappeared altogether. "No one in the Program has

heard from him," Pat said. "That's just like him. But then someone told me he was in the hospital . . . "

I wondered what this might mean, and what it might mean
about Pat's health, but quickly brushed the thought aside. In a
wry tone Pat continued telling me about one of his boyfriend's
previous disappearances. It was late, and I let myself grow mesmerized by Pat's world. Suddenly he looked at his watch. His
friend Larry was expecting us for late-night tea, he said. "I've
told Larry all about you. Larry and I are really tight."

"OK," I said. "Sure." I might have hoped to get home and
into bed, ending this day as soon as possible, yet for some reason I was determined to see this side trip through to the end.

PAT POINTED out a gay bar on the way to the car.

"So, any boys there?" I asked.

"Tonight?" Pat shrugged. We decided to walk through. On
my last visit to San Jose my brother and I had gone to a neighborhood place called A Tinker's Damn, butt of countless
schoolyard jokes. I had gone in to break that spell of fear and
shame, but inside I saw no one I would ever want to meet, and
Ken and I sat alone in a corner, leaving before we even finished
our beers. Now I wanted to see if this downtown bar was any
better.

It was dark and huge and nearly empty. "Sunday night," said
Pat knowingly. A few guys in ill-fitting jeans sat around one of
the bars. "Alky night," said Pat even more knowingly. In the
next room, *Mommie Dearest* was playing on a giant video screen,
Faye Dunaway screaming at the daughter.

We hurried out the sliding door that led onto an empty patio. "I don't know why anyone thinks that movie is funny," I murmured. I was beginning to feel more and more strange. Out on the street again I put on a therapist's voice. "That wasn't a very affirming experience, Patrick." But the joke was lost on him.

PAT'S FRIEND Larry lived at the very top of an elaborate gray Victorian, in a sort of tower, reached by its own wooden staircase. The house was surrounded by tall trees.

Larry, tall with frizzy red hair, greeted us in a mandala T-shirt and a string of beads. He and Pat hugged, Larry running his pinkish hands over Pat's back with New Age affection. "How ya doin', brother?" Larry cooed. "How ya holdin' up?"

It occurred to me that I hadn't been very understanding tonight about Pat's current troubles. In the same instant, I looked around the apartment and saw that Larry had covered every wall with shiny blue plastic.

"Ah, Cliff," Larry said, shaking my hand and looking deeply into my eyes. "Do you want some of Larry's special tea?"

"It's great," said Pat smoothly, seating himself on a black vinyl beanbag chair. He seemed quite at home already, and I supposed he wouldn't mind staying here if he got evicted from his apartment.

With extreme precision, as if preparing a controlled substance, Larry measured water into the teakettle and carefully blended his tea from several bags of herbs. "Yeah, Pat and I go way back," he said, placing mugs on a small Formica table. He sat down and looked at me intently. His eyes were unfixed. "We knew each other in our other lives," he said, as if testing to see how I would respond. "We can't get rid of each other." He laughed a little too uproariously and turned to Pat. "No, you can't get rid of me, can you?"

Larry's eyes closed in silent, knowing laughter. I turned away and saw a dead Christmas tree in the corner of the room. It must have been there nearly a year. "That's our tree!" said Pat, following my eye, and he laughed his old, hacking drug laugh, a toneless stuttering.

Larry poured from a brown clay teapot. He explained that Pat's course now was troubled but inevitable. He looked at me intently again. "Have you ever heard of spirit guides?" He himself was smiling like a beneficent spirit.

"I guess I really am in California now," I managed to say.

"Yeah, you don't hear about this stuff back east too much," Larry agreed.

The tea tasted strange, sweet in my throat but not on my tongue. I looked up and saw that even the ceiling was covered in plastic. As Larry explained spirit guides to me, I began to feel as though I had been drawn through a narrow glass pipette, up and up, into this strange, blue-plastic world.

"Larry can see auras," said Pat, stirring his tea.

"Can you see mine?" I asked, ready to indulge myself with a possible new form of vanity.

Larry looked closely at my head.

"Mine's *purple*," said Pat, pronouncing the word like a monster character he had made up in high school.

Larry continued looking at my head, knitting his brow. "I can't be sure. . . . Greenish, maybe . . . "

WHEN I GOT HOME I realized my raincoat was missing. I searched the trunk, under the seats. I was quite certain that I had left it on the backseat when Pat and I went to Larry's. It must have been stolen.

Swearing, I went into the house. It was well after midnight and my parents were in bed, behind a door in which my father had recently installed a dead bolt to keep away burglars. I went down the hall to the kitchen to call Pat, just in case I might have left my raincoat at his place or Larry's. Turning on the light, I looked where the phone should have been and saw that it, too, was gone.

My father, I remembered then, disconnected the phone each night and took it into his locked bedroom. He said that otherwise robbers might take the kitchen phone off the hook, preventing him from using the extension by the bed.

I stood staring a moment at the metal plate on the off-white stucco wall, and the empty jack. At the mercy of my parents again, and no ally in sight. "Oh, dih," I said.

I went back out to the car and looked again, feeling under the seats, leaning my head all the way into the trunk. I half expected my raincoat to reappear, like some sort of playful sprite. I shut the trunk and stood in the dank orange lamplight, looking dismally down the deserted street. Why hadn't I made sure the doors were locked, or put it safely in the trunk? All the bizarre and unpleasant events of the weekend now seemed to have added up, some critical mass had been reached, and the doom feeling was upon me. It seemed like my soul had been carried off with my raincoat.

I recalled the first time I wore it, just a few weeks before, on a day out of the city with Gabby, my best friend in New York. I had gone out to see her, at her parents' house in New Jersey, because her grandmother had just died.

Gabby met me at the bus and we drove to an apple orchard nearby. She didn't want to go back to her relatives yet, and we walked in the drizzle down through the short trees, the apples ripe and dusky between the leaves.

This was, before my brother got sick, the closest I had yet come to a death. Gabby talked about her grandmother, how much she loved her, how through her mother's various tribulations it was basically her grandmother who had raised her. And I absently fingered the insides of my coat's new, satin pockets . . .

Waking me from these thoughts, a car full of loud teenagers barreled down my parents' street, squealing around the corner.

"My raincoat," I murmured.

Then I was angry again. "Damn. Why didn't I lock that car?"

3.

The bluffs sloped off steeply and then dropped straight to the sea. Dull, heathery succulents and scrubby bushes covered the rocky ground, with tufts of white or yellow wildflowers.

Below, the huge rocks were dark brown, stained darker by the water, which itself was inky, white as it crashed into bits, and milky blue-green where it boiled in deep pools.

It was just after sundown, and there were no clouds in the sky. Our cabin, weathered gray wood, stood in a loose group of shacks on the edge of the bluffs. Otherwise it was empty coast, north and south. Puffs of gray smoke rose from the small cabin chimneys and from outdoor barbecues.

I found Cathy and her friend Albert huddled around our own grill, where chicken pieces were broiling. They were talking again about how hard it is to find a lover, our favorite topic since we set out from Berkeley that morning. Earlier in the afternoon, just after we arrived, there we were, the three of us kneeling on the floor of our cabin—in the middle of nowhere—reading the gay personal ads from a San Francisco paper.

As I approached the fire, Cathy began improvising new ads. "Lesbian graduate student, loves candlelit dinners and long walks on the beach, dropping trash behind us."

I took out my camera. "Your photo gets mine," I said, aiming and shooting. "No fats, no fems."

Albie waved his chicken fork in greeting. "Unstable Cliffs!" he said, referring to the signs all around the campsite.

"So, your parents were married—what?—fifty years?" said Cathy, poking the chicken with her spatula, "Tell us all about love."

"Fifty years of solitude," I said.

Cathy's high, bobbing, sympathetic laughter rang across the bluffs. "So you can't tell me how to find a girlfriend?"

I said I guessed not. Cathy and I had known each other since college, and we had slept together off and on as recently as a year before. Somehow that didn't feel right anymore, and I didn't think it would happen on this trip. But the transition made me feel a little awkward and wounded anyway.

"I kissed a boy at a bar last week," I said with mock pride.

"Slut!" said Albie and Cathy, one after the other.

"For I will make you fishers of *men!*" Albie added.

Slyly I watched his wide, rosy face as he turned the chicken deftly with a fork, his new studded bracelet gleaming, and I concluded once again that I wasn't attracted to him.

"A perfect stranger. I *did* feel like a slut," I confessed. I took the spatula from Cathy, patted each piece of chicken, and told them about my various disaster dates over the previous two years. "There was that guy who only wanted to write me pornographic letters. And then there was the one at Boy Bar who said he was really nervous talking to me because he just quit smoking pot . . . " The subject quickly began to depress me. "Oh, well," I said with false and abrupt cheerfulness.

I turned and looked out from under the cabin eaves at the bluffs, yellowy and glowing in the still-bright sky. The ocean could be heard, far below, an under-roar that made me anxious. I stared a minute more, trying to capture some sense of beauty and ecstasy that I always expected from a vacation in California. But at the moment it was a trick of self-hypnosis I couldn't manage.

Behind me, the grill sizzled. "Almost done," Albie said. Cathy began making chicken noises.

AFTER DINNER the moon came up and we picked our way down the cliffside, huddled together so we wouldn't fall, following a thin, gray, pebbly moonlit trail. When we reached the bottom, we ran across the short, flat beach, spreading out with the centrifugal force of sudden speed, released.

Then we stopped, three points on the sand, and looked out at the loud ocean, the white foam glowing before the moon. A breeze came off the cliffs, bringing the ruddy odor of dry California scrub. "Wow," said Cathy, spreading her arms and letting them drop. Albie went and sat down on a huge log, and Cathy and I followed. We leaned on our knees, chins in hands, like three children, watching the roaring, big ocean in the dark.

"Shit, it's too bad I have to leave tomorrow," I said. I had just gotten here, and already I was supposed to go see my friend Mike in Santa Cruz the next day. There just didn't seem to be enough time for everything I wanted to do this week, and I was feeling like an overscheduled executive. I wanted to stay here, and yet I wanted to spend the entire week with Mike, too.

"Big wave," said Albie, pointing. As we watched, an especially high edge of white dropped, and there was a huge crash. The water flowed in to within a few feet of us.

Later, Cathy and I lay side by side in our two sleeping bags, Albie asleep in the other room of the cabin. This was our first chance to really talk since I picked her up in Berkeley. In the candlelight I lay tapping my foot rapidly against the wooden wall.

Cathy told me about her latest difficulties with her parents, who still would not accept that she was gay. "My mother wrote me saying it was like I had joined some weird religious sect."

Cathy was silent, and I turned to see her small nose in profile, her short, blond hair fanned out above her forehead. She had had severe eye problems since birth, and her parents had taken her through a dozen or more operations. As a child with very thick glasses and a wandering eye, she endured terrible teasing at school and had always relied on her parents more than other children might. Her eyes were dark now in the candlelight. "No, Mom and Dad haven't come around yet," she said wryly.

No wonder I'm not out to my parents, I thought to myself.

"How's your brother?" Cathy asked.

Over the past several months I had kept Cathy up to date about Ken's health. I told her now the news about his T-cell count. "His doctor said it's only a matter of time before he gets sick."

She sighed. "Oh, boy." She stroked my shoulder. At that moment she must have understood the seriousness of it all better than I did; I was right in the middle of it, and not wanting to see much. Her concern, combined with the history of our touching—her hand on my shoulder now—made me very nervous. I began to wonder again if I would ever settle down on this trip, if I could enjoy myself for even a second.

I told her that Ken was weighing the risks of going on AZT. "I definitely don't know what he should do," I said, feeling exhausted. "He's not sick yet."

Cathy replied that she guessed it was up to Ken, and he would decide. I tried to agree convincingly. I forced myself to stop tapping my foot and stared up at the little pitch-black window, at the reflection of our guttering candle.

"You're the only one who knows?" Cathy asked.

I nodded.

She said only, "Hmm."

The ocean was still roaring somewhere. "I don't know who else he can tell," I said. Perhaps I didn't want to give up my place as sole confidante, which might have seemed like another loss to his illness. "He's not even out to my parents. You can't really talk to them about anything emotional, let alone that. Maybe he could tell my sister Carol, but I don't know what she's going to do about it, either." I was getting mad now. "But then I don't know what anyone is supposed to do about it."

4.

With scarcely any sleep, the next day I took the freeway to Santa Cruz to see Mike. Just passing out of San Francisco, I glimpsed the late afternoon sun, bright yellow on a row of bright houses on a hill, and a tear came to my eye. But the big road quickly turned, and the moment was gone.

Mike's face is wide and square, his nose pink and translucent, slightly hooked. His hair is curly, a flat blond color, and he has a wide, thin smile, and prominent but rounded cheeks.

Even approaching thirty, he liked to make faces, and if you asked him he would still do "the Sloth," taking on a particularly passive expression and moving his arms and fingers with excruciating slowness. The humor in Mike's imitations was always his ability to keep them up long after anyone else would have stopped, or any reasonable audience had lost interest—still moving his arms as slowly as the hands of a clock, and slowly, slowly turning his torso sideways, his big head dialing gradually upward, staring intently at a fixed point, as if he were hanging upside down from some jungle branch.

It took Mike more than ten years to finish college. When we were in school together, I used to find him near the end of the term in his dorm room, sitting on his bed, playing his recorder. He could do that for days, failing one course after another. His slow academic progress was of no particular concern to him and never led to any particular crisis. He blended into the laid-back, late-hippie world of Santa Cruz, where there were no grades and the failing marks never showed up on his transcript. He took yoga and clerked in the library; he dropped out for a while; he took a few more classes, dropped a few; he changed his major several times; he let most of his incompletes lapse. Then for three or four years he had only to write his thesis and he would graduate, but still he lingered, as if his decade in school were some rare and sweet and ineffable work of art that he could not bear to finish.

His father had been a butcher and meat-faced afternoon drinker; he died of a heart attack when Mike was nineteen. When Mike was two, his father's second business failed—a meat market bankrolled on the mother's savings—and his father ran away to Lake Tahoe, taking Mike with him. For two days no one knew where they were. The father drank and gambled, and probably he left the small child alone for long periods in the motel room. Whatever happened, Mike's mother said that Mike was different—quieter—after he and his father returned.

Mike is very shy, tallish, his body stiff and a little awkward. He speaks rather formally in a deep, nasal voice like an actor or a radio announcer. I've known him since sixth grade, when he invited me to swim in his backyard pool after drama class. Of my three best friends during high school—Pat, Wayne, and Mike—only Mike turned out to be straight. We grew very close my senior year of college and during the summer after I graduated, when I lived in a house just up a short hill from him in Santa Cruz. When Mike visited me there, he used to climb through the big, low window of my room, skipping the front door.

I think of Mike more or less as a brother.

OF ALL MY WEEK'S visits, I was most anxious about this one with Mike, which I was afraid would be too brief. Since Mike was still in school, and his life had therefore changed little since I moved to New York seven years before, it seemed deceptively simple for us to fall into our old college intimacy. Yet I hadn't seen him in almost a year, and as we sat in his backyard together suddenly I felt like I hardly knew him. I took pictures of him at the redwood table, almost just to see what he looked like.

We went to our old supermarket and bought the wine we always bought, and then we came home and settled down in Mike's dark basement kitchen to cook our meal. I told him then about my brother. "I've never known anyone who was sick before this," I said. "This is all really new." Perhaps I hoped for some insight from Mike, since he had already lost his father, but he offered none. I told him I was worried, and then I fell silent.

In fact, neither Mike nor I was in the same place we were seven years before. Most notably, I was a gay man now. Seven years earlier, I was just getting to know my only real girlfriend, Alix—who back then happened to live in Mike's very room, in this very house, in Santa Cruz.

Soon dinner was ready, and we sat down at the small table. I began eating, searching for a topic of conversation. Mike politely asked what I had done this week besides camping with Cathy. "Oh, God, I saw Pat Heaney," I said with relief.

Mike was my only friend in California who also knew Pat, so now at last I was able to explain fully the bizarre Sunday evening I had spent with him.

"I haven't seen Pat in . . . ," Mike said. "Well, you remember that one time." He raised one eyebrow, a half-exaggerated gesture of scandal, but also half serious.

"What? What?" I said. I knew exactly what incident he was talking about, but I wanted to hear it again.

A few years before, when Pat was still doing drugs, he once "crashed" with Mike for a week in Santa Cruz. Mike came home one morning—he was working graveyard at the Wrigley's gum factory—and found Pat passed out on the bed in the spare room, surrounded by dildos and porno magazines.

I laughed, but a bit nervously. "Well, Pat always wore his heart on his sleeve. . . . What did you do?"

"I think I just sort of backed out of the apartment and went downtown for breakfast. When I got home again, Pat was up, and neither of us ever mentioned it."

I chuckled. "I'm trying to imagine the look on your face when you walked in on him," I said.

This topic led rather naturally to sex, and we compared notes on being single. He had broken up with his girlfriend Roslyn a year or so before, after staying with her perhaps two years longer than he intended. We agreed that it certainly was very hard to find someone you liked, and harder still to tell if you were even ready for it, or if it wasn't happening because actually you didn't want it . . .

In this way we passed the meal, making our way through an entire bottle of wine. "I can't believe we ate all that," I said, leaning over to look at the empty salad bowl and the nearly empty pasta colander. "Weren't we supposed to save some?"

One of Mike's housemates would be getting home soon from work, and Mike had promised to keep some dinner for him. Mike smiled at me devilishly. I knew he didn't care much for that housemate.

"*Hyet,*" I said, an imitation of a hiccup and, more precisely, our secret sound of conspiratorial glee that went back to when we were twelve. "Hyet, hyet."

We fell to making noises then, regressing deliciously. Mike began barking like a dog, and then grunting like some lost sea monster. His eyes were wild and he clawed the air with one withered-looking hand. I threw my head back, laughing. When I looked again, Mike began his low, trailing-off chuckle, slightly embarrassed. He looked to the side nervously and took another sip of wine.

This was the dense and many-yeared, multistoried past we shared, the sense of common history that I had missed all week since Ken didn't show up in San Jose—a layered, warm sensation that was both delicate and profound, made up of countless repeated moments, well-known gestures, running jokes. I had known Cathy only since college, but with Mike it went back to when I was twelve. Of course with my brother the sense of shared history went far deeper, and this was the rarest and most irreplaceable thing, the most shattering of losses when Ken died. I lost my own self as it was so thoroughly known, and the child's soul of me wasn't sure who was gone then, me or Ken.

Mike restored his face to its normal, angelic calm, and I laughed again. But then uncertainty, or some sudden recollection of myself, pulled me up sharply, like a fish on a line. I cleared my throat, moved to take my dish to the sink.

"Yes," said Mike absently, rising, as if my action had been a question or a reminder.

We stood over the sink. There was no dish towel, so I just watched Mike wash, sometimes repositioning pots in the drainer. He placed a dented, shiny aluminum pot in the stack.

"So, I kissed a boy at a bar last week," I said, repeating exactly what I had told Cathy and Albie two days before. I still seemed to be working on the incident in my mind.

"Right in the bar?" said Mike evenly. I watched his profile closely to see if he minded talking about these things. He didn't seem to.

"I don't know, I just went really wild!" I cried.

Mike said that was good. "I wish I could break out a little," he declared. This was a quintessential Mike thing to say, and I found its familiarity comforting.

"How would you break out?" I asked eagerly.

He said he wanted to go to India, and he was thinking of moving to Japan.

"Really?" I remembered the last time he went traveling, perhaps a year after his father died. He sold his car and went to Europe, planning a half-year journey. But Mike wasn't cut out for traveling by himself; he got lonely and came home after only a month. "Yeah, I wish I were more wild," I said. Next I made the inevitable fearful connection. "Though I guess maybe it's lucky I haven't been."

There was a pause. Then Mike asked, "Did Ken . . . ?"

"I think he screwed around a lot, yeah." I stared at the dripping pile of dishes and pans. With the arrogance of the fortunate, I was blaming my brother for what had happened to him. But actually I had no idea how much Ken "screwed around." And whether it was "a lot" or "a little," under this train of logic it could only be "too much." Quickly I added, to soften the remark: "Well, but who knew?"

Mike dried his hands on his pants. "Yeah, who knew?"

MY BROTHER and I had drifted apart for a while, after he came out to me when I was in college. This was the period when I still went out with women, and I was a little scared of him. I remember one visit home when he and I had planned to go to San

Francisco for the day. Then Mike called while we were eating breakfast. He said he was also in town, and I suggested he come right over. When I got off the phone, Ken said, "I thought we were going to San Francisco."

I hedged. "I thought it was tentative." Ken turned to his muffin and began buttering it attentively, frowning. I said, "I thought you'd want to go to bars and—" My mother was sitting right there eating her soft-boiled egg. "—and meet people, and I thought you'd just as soon go by yourself."

It would be hilarious, if it weren't so painful, that I could think cruising in bars in broad daylight could be my brother's only possible agenda in San Francisco.

Ken's face was redder than usual. He put down his butter knife. "I thought we'd go to the pier or the park or something. I thought we were spending the day together."

"Oh. All right," I said smoothly, as if this had been the simplest of misunderstandings. "I'll call Mike back. I'm sorry. When do you want to leave?"

I SLEPT BADLY on the couch in Mike's living room. The same dream over and over. In the family room, playing with a balloon, Ken asked me a question I didn't understand. I answered tentatively, incorrectly, and he very sarcastically asked the question again.

I stood up and started yelling. My parents sat on the couch, impassive or glaring, I'm not sure which. "I didn't understand the question!" I shouted. "You always do that! You always do that!" He retreated down the hall. I knew it was only his own fear of the question itself that made him repeat it sarcastically.

I called after him, "You always do that!"

AROUND NOON, Mike and I went to Capitola, the next town down the coast. I had to go back to San Jose that same afternoon, and that prospect hung over me.

But we bought ice-cream cones and walked to the pier, licking happily enough, saying nothing. "God, I have to go back," I said at last.

"I know, I know," said Mike. I didn't need to explain to him my fear of wilting under my parents' spell, and he felt pretty much the same way about his own family. But the vague, enervating dread I was feeling went beyond that.

This day was, as it turned out, only a month before my brother would first get really sick—before I could have known anything of what it would be like for him to be so sick, or how it would feel to be losing him; and then to lose him; and then to have lost him.

I was always hoping, and always being caught unawares. Just one month later, the day after Thanksgiving, I would call Ken to confirm my plans for seeing him at Christmas, and I would learn that he had had pneumonia that week and nearly died. He had just gotten out of the hospital that morning.

And he would recover splendidly from that bout, but in little more than a year he would be in the hospital again. His mind was going rapidly by then, and he was so weak he would fall

asleep on the telephone. His groggy answers gave way to silence. "Ken?" I called to him, hanging on to the receiver. "Are
you there?" I wanted to bring him back, as if he were only sleep-
walking toward death and somehow I had to wake him and turn
his sleepy body back toward survival. Don't give up! Weren't we
in this together? . . . But he must have dropped the phone on
the bed, and I heard only my own voice echoing out to him, sil-
very and metallic on the line.

"Ken! *Ken?. . .* Ken."

I DIDN'T KNOW any of this, standing on the pier that day with
my childhood friend Mike, early November, 1987, only a year
and a half before. Though it's almost as if I did, running from
something and searching all week for what seemed my lost soul,
for some sense of wholeness or well-being that seemed to have
been stolen along with my raincoat. But there on the pier with
Mike, just an hour before it was time for me to go back to my
family and San Jose, I suddenly relaxed. I seemed to have found
myself, to have come to life again.

We finished our ice creams and walked together down near
the end of the pier, where there were fishermen. A single seal
barked somewhere below, echoing in the pilings. Leaning on
the rail, I looked at the wooded cliffs across the bay, glowing in
a gray light, and then out to sea. Between the even layer of
clouds, a wedge of blue had opened, a delta, fluorescent and reflected brightly down in the calm water—which under the white
clouds was capable of being very green, fully itself. I thought I
had never seen such beautiful colors—the dusky green, and the

blue reflected. I breathed in deeply, and let out the air again, feeling my own, sudden, fragile wholeness. It gave me hope, though not of any specific kind.

Shouts came from down the pier.

"Man caught a fish," said Mike, nodding in that direction.

I looked. The quivering pole was swung back over the railing, and the fish hung flopping and silver, a twisting flatness on the line—a small, round fish, size of your hand.

Another man, Irish looking, bald and squat, took the fish from the hook. He threw it down on the pier, where it flipped here and there on the gray, weathered boards. It nearly flipped under the rail and over the edge, but the Irish-looking man kicked it back to the center of the pier, chuckling.

Then he picked it up and held it out to the gulls fluttering by the concession stand. "Hey, come 'ere. Come 'ere!" he called to them. The other men stood around laughing genially.

I guess they don't want it, I said to myself. Yes, it was too small. But the fish was so remarkable. And they had caught it. How could they not want it?

Absorbed, I completely forgot my troubles, past or impending. The Irishman waved the shiny fish at one braver gull who had landed just a few yards away. "Hey, Joseph, come 'ere, Joseph," cried the man. The others laughed louder. The seagull stood on one orange, webbed foot, and then another, frowning. "C'mon, you want it, Joseph?"

Joseph made a single, running dive for the fish, but missed, and in the same motion flew off, arcing up over the concession stand.

The Irishman cried out with mock disdain. The show over, the others began to return to their poles and lines. The Irishman stood squat and defeated for a moment, his back to the rail. No one was watching him now but me.

Shrugging, he suddenly tossed the fish over his shoulder, like spilled salt.

I saw the silver thing go flying down into the bay. I watched the place where it landed. Now it lay flat and shining in the water, just under the surface. Surely Joseph would get it now, I thought.

But then it quivered, flashed almost imperceptibly, and was gone. It seemed almost to have sunk. But it was alive. It had swum free, out of all danger.

Love Can't Hurt Me

1.

"MY MOTHER was a wonderful person, a wonderful person," my own mother begins. I've asked her to tell me, once more, the story of my grandmother's death. "So full of love. All the children on the block used to call her Auntie Sawyer."

My grandmother was in fact the reason my parents left the Christian Science Church.

"How long was she sick?" I ask.

"A long time. It may have been yours. Headaches, terrible pain in the legs." My mother stares at her empty mug. "Then she was in a car accident, when she was traveling with Grandpa. This was just after the war ended."

My grandfather was an auditor for Sherwin Williams, and he traveled around the Midwest visiting plants to check the books. The accident took place on such a journey.

"He took Grandma on his business trips?" I ask. For a moment I imagine they had a particularly romantic marriage.

"Because she was so sick by then," my mother says. "He had to take care of her."

He and my grandmother were on their way to the next factory. It was a long drive. My grandfather had been up most of the night in the motel—praying for my grandmother, trying to keep her comfortable. That afternoon on the narrow, monotonous highway through cornfields, as my grandmother slept soundly in the backseat, my grandfather grew drowsy. His eyes drooped closed. He drove the car off the road.

He suffered only minor injuries. But my grandmother was thrown against the chrome handle of the back door. (I note to myself the odd correspondences to Ken's first accident: *highway, backseat, door handle*. But the story rushes forward.) "She cut her ear very badly," my mother says, "and Grandpa had to take her to the nearest hospital. They took one look at her and could see she was diabetic."

After the doctor had dressed my grandmother's ear, he wouldn't let her leave. She was given a bed and put on insulin.

She stayed perhaps two weeks, and her health improved a great deal. Her disease was explained to her. She was given the name of a doctor in Chicago and instructions about diet. She returned home with my grandfather.

Here the story grows worn and scratchy, like a record played too many times. It's so familiar that now my mother doesn't even bother to tell the rest.

Apparently when my grandparents got back to Chicago, a fellow church member baked my grandmother a get-well cake. Perhaps it was even waiting on the doorstep when they returned from the distant hospital, or perhaps she received it a few days later. I wonder if this turning point was chocolate, or lemon-filled with white frosting. In any case, all at once my grandmother resolved to ignore everything the doctors had told her. She would eat the cake, this gift to her, no matter what.

"Love can't hurt me," she said.

This has always been the end of the story, and as a child I thought my grandmother died then and there, because of the sweet cake—like Babar's king eating bad mushrooms.

"And after the cake?" I ask my mother now, suddenly realizing there must be more.

She shrugs. "After that she pretty much just got worse and worse."

"She wouldn't see a doctor anymore?"

My mother begins clearing the dishes. "No. Or stop eating sweets."

"When did she die?"

"A few months later, I think."

My mother isn't used to telling the story this way, and I refrain from asking the exact circumstances of the end. Anyway, the key has always been that poison cake, quivering like fate on

a dining-room table—the warning unheeded; the mistaken conviction; the missed chance. And most important, repeated over
and over with a shake of the head, looming in history, was what
my grandmother said that pivotal day, when she decided once
and for all to ignore reason, to live by what is unseen, to throw
away her life and eat.

Mind must be found superior to all the beliefs of the five corporeal
senses, and able to destroy all ills. Sickness, writes Mary Baker Eddy,
is a belief, which must be annihilated by the divine Mind.

When she was twenty-nine—about the time that my grandmother died—my mother had to have all her teeth pulled. Pre-
sumably she had never seen a dentist when she was growing up,
and I imagine there must have been years of toothaches. It isn't
something she talks about.

Earlier, my mother wasn't allowed eyeglasses until she was in
high school. When a teacher discovered that she couldn't read
the blackboard, her parents sent her first to a Christian Science
practitioner. The diagnosis: she didn't see the good in other
people.

"I went around for weeks trying to think good thoughts
about everyone," my mother says. "I still couldn't see the
board." Eventually her father broke down and took her to get
her first pair of glasses.

My mother had long rejected Christian Science by the time
I was born, and I heard this wry story often. But though she had
successfully converted sickness from belief to reality, certain
other complaints of the five corporeal senses never quite gained

my mother's recognition. She had inherited an almost infinitely flexible logic, shared by my father (whose parents also were Christian Scientist), one that could virtually transform reality. And she had inherited a belief in the power of that logic. *There is no life, truth, intelligence, nor substance in matter. All is infinite Mind and its infinite manifestation.* My mother's mind could, indeed, turn the plainest facts on their heads.

She likes to tell a story of how my oldest brother, Paul, came home from high school one day following a counseling session with his teacher. Paul, who was often in trouble, said his teacher had explained to him the special problems that middle children face. Paul is the exact center of the family, the third of five kids.

My mother replied that she would hear none of this mumbo jumbo. Paul had nothing to complain about, she said, because in fact he wasn't the middle child at all. "Ken wasn't born until you were five, so until then you were the youngest child," she told him. "And you were the first boy, so after Ken arrived, you were the oldest."

Question.—Does brain think, and do nerves feel, and is there intelligence in matter?

Answer.—No, not if God is true and mortal man a liar. The assertion that there can be pain or pleasure in matter is erroneous.

Of the civil-rights movement, for instance, my mother used to say, "Those people aren't unhappy. We lived in New Orleans. We used to see them, sitting out on their porches. They were perfectly happy until someone came along and told them they weren't."

ILLNESS, HOWEVER, could gain my mother's undivided attention. I remember the gifts she brought me one afternoon when I
had a cold—two new toys, and not even my birthday: a huge picture puzzle, and a kit to make a horse from felt and wood. The
horse seemed the rarest and most urgent of treasures, and I
stayed up well past bedtime assembling it. I didn't want to stop!
My mother made only perfunctory warnings of the late hour,
while in fevered industry, sitting at a TV tray in the family room,
a blanket over my knees, I glued and snipped, found the eyes of
the horse in the box, shook them and made them move, attached
them to the sides of his head. It's a sick-time vigor I've felt ever
since, a life of the mind that's possible only with a runny nose and
a temperature. My mother sent me to school the next morning,
figuring I must be recovered. But I wasn't, and I coughed and
sniffled through the day, furious with her, planning what to say
that would make her feel the most guilty when I got home.

When Ken was in high school, I'd watch him stumble into
the kitchen for breakfast and announce to my mother, his eyes
shining with complicity, that he had a sore throat. She, barely re-
pressing a smile, would tell him he could stay home and "rest."
We had moved twice in the past two years, and Ken was on his
third high school. Discussing this obvious fact would have been
futile, but as if my mother needed discretion in thwarting her
own authority, she allowed Ken his imaginary illnesses.

In seventh grade, swallowed up by new and lonely adversity,
I began using the sore-throat trick myself. But unlike Ken, I
knew no restraint, and after three days in a row, my mother said

that I had to go to school. "You can't keep doing this," she said, looking at me very seriously. I could only protest, to no avail, that I really wasn't feeling well. I knew no other way to explain that school had become a cave, that each cloudy morning the cold, open-air hallways were darker than the day before, and that I preferred the warm, solitary deadness of the house and my bed, the sad and absolute silence after the garage door had slammed shut and my mother had left for work.

Twenty years later, I find in illness the same combination of escape and despair. Even with the mildest cold, I'm very much in my own world, a sorry and persecuted exile, but also free from everyday compromises. After a day in bed I can hardly imagine I have a job to go to, tasks to perform, money to earn. The illness seems the most real: headaches, Kleenex, tea, sore throats, naps—naps most of all, a world of drowsiness, sitting up in bed reading, lying in bed, extra blankets, the changing light behind paper blinds, waves of sleep, odd dreams, boredom, and my own thoughts.

Perhaps I still communicate lost truths to myself through illness. Groggy and sniffling, I imagine I'm going through some transformation, into a cocoon to emerge a newer creature. In the drowsy, endless afternoon I might dream, for the first time, that I'm a sailor . . .

I first went into therapy, years ago, because I got sick all the time—a cold at least once a month. I would have to stay home from work a day at least—a week or more for a bad one. Finally I got mono and had to stay in bed for three weeks; for a month after that I could work only until two each day. It was my boss then, an elderly newspaperman, who had to sit me down and say to me seriously, "You can't keep doing this."

That spring, as the first reports of homosexuals and failed immunity appeared in the *New York Times,* I read them intently. I had already thought a lot about my immune system, as well as homosexuality. I had a girlfriend at the time and had been with a man only briefly, a year before. Frequent colds: it was as if I had been given a limited immune disorder, in payment for my limited activity.

My girlfriend indulged my illnesses, bringing me chicken soup and getting into bed with me. I grew rail thin from the mono; she said it was "sexy." That summer she moved away, back to California, and I managed to get my illnesses down to once every two months. The unraveling of many more lost truths would be necessary before I could do better than that. Still, I tend to think of illness as tempting, like a mild drug. I want release, and perhaps to hurt myself too. In turn, I feel cursed when I get sick, like I brought it all on myself. And when I haven't had a cold for several months, I pat myself on the back. I feel like I've accomplished something.

And if an illness were serious, life threatening? What becomes then of the old game of escape and despair, the pixilated illusion of mastery, so easy with a flu or a toothache: you soon get better; you have won the fight; you are blessed. But if sickness proves stronger than you are?

For years my mother sought to unlearn that disease is all in the mind. Frequently she made jokes of phrases like "mental malpractice" and "there is no power in matter." Somehow the ideas got transmitted anyway.

2.

It was the day before Christmas. Ken had almost died, and I didn't want to reach San Diego.

The tiny plane dipped and bucked. If I clenched hard, my stomach would stop its sloshing for just a minute. I saw the plane crashing: The End. Already the flight had been delayed more than an hour because of this wind, and I'd had to call Ken's house to let my parents know I'd be late. Was it safe now? Sometimes the craft seemed almost to be flying sideways. The coastline rolled below, the water twinkling too near, not the splendid, harmless distance I knew from flights on bigger planes.

I nearly laughed when I first stepped on board—just a single row of passengers on either side. I had never seen that before. The little seats were thinly padded and low-slung, and the ceiling was low and curved. The airline's bold logo seemed absurd on such a small craft, its slender nose forlorn on the windy tarmac. As if San Diego were the ends of the earth, I thought. Or as if going to see Ken now—viewing up close the tragedy that was yet unfolding—required some kind of humbling ritual, like the samurai crawling into the Japanese teahouse, or a camel passing through the eye of the needle.

"Of course love can hurt you," I said to myself. "You old bag. Everyone knows that."

With a series of feints and shudders, the little plane landed.

THERE HAD BEEN some question of my being picked up at the airport. My mother, engrossed in the details of caring for Ken, didn't think she would be able to get away. But I wanted someone to come and get me, now of all times. "Couldn't Dad come by himself?" I asked, but I knew the answer. "What if Dad got lost?" my mother said. Without her navigation skills, he would never find his way back to Ken's house. And I myself feared this most rare event, a transaction between just my father and me, without my mother's mediation.

In the end, both of them were waiting for me at the curb. Things had settled down enough for Ken to be alone in the house for a little while. I hugged my mother and then my father with a new and tentative warmth, quickly releasing, uneasy with the survivor's sudden knowledge of how precious we were to each other. We got into the old Mercury. "He's getting better every day," my mother said. A spirit of busy hope had taken over her gestures. Her head tilted from side to side as she talked, looking ahead, interrupting herself to point the next turn to my father. "He should be back at work in a month."

I glanced at the wide jetway that directly crossed the airport boulevard. Cars would have to stop for a jumbo jet making its way to the hangars. The plane would seem like a huge creature out of its element, I thought, in the wrong world or the wrong time. The two kinds of roads—cars and jumbo jets—seemed to have transgressed in crossing.

"He's taking a nap now," my mother continued. "He should be up by the time we get home. . . . Feel that wind." A strong gust had just buffeted the car.

"That's what I was just in," I said, looking up at the sky, as if moving air were visible. "So Ken's been pretty much up and around?"

"Oh, yes," said my mother knowingly.

I was vaguely resentful of being conveyed by my parents into the heart of my brother's illness, a sanctum where I myself formerly officiated. The highways and streets of San Diego, a city I had never before visited, were a carefully constructed maze, shaded by palm and eucalyptus, and only my mother knew the way.

Though he had been desperately ill, Ken didn't call me when he went into the hospital. It was my mother who answered his phone, surprising me, the day after Thanksgiving, and she was the one who gave me the news. I wondered why she herself hadn't called me either. I had to ask her if I could speak to Ken, who had just gotten home that morning, and she said she'd go see if he was awake. He did come to the phone, but we talked only briefly.

A few days later I received a letter from him. Aside from quick greetings on birthday cards, this was perhaps the first letter he had ever written me. *I've felt closer to Mom and Dad than ever before, and over the past few days we have been able to talk more openly and honestly than we ever have. I have told them that I'm gay, which they have accepted fully. I have also told them about being in Narcotics Anonymous, and my struggle with addiction to marijuana. . . .*

I slid the paper carefully back in its envelope, mortified by this sudden and untoward intimacy with my parents. Ken seemed to have humbled himself too completely, and I felt as though I had watched him undress in public. I wished that he had drawn the line somewhere. Gay—OK, I thought, you have AIDS, it's unavoidable. But addicted to pot—no, don't tell them that. And yet I longed to participate in that flickering spell that seemed to hang over him and my parents, far away in San Diego—I imagined the three of them under a yellow light in an otherwise darkened room—Ken suddenly sharing all his secrets, and my parents suddenly able to listen.

The fiery comet, passing so near my brother, had made my mother and father understanding, and my brother honest. But no such near catastrophe had touched me. What would make my parents, at long last, understand me—and me, at long last, able to fall into their loving arms?

SHYLY MY BROTHER and I hugged in the little kitchen. His cheeks were ruddy but drawn, and his mustache seemed to float an inch away from the gauntness of his face. I averted my gaze to the cabinet just behind his head. "What a flight," I said, re-sorting to a thirteen-year-old's gagging gesture. Ken chuckled.

"I'll put your bag in the front room," offered my father, his efficient back disappearing through the arched doorway.

"Yeah, those little planes," said Ken. I watched him pour himself a glass of water from a big jug. "Only plain water," he explained, toasting me. "Filtered. Or herb tea—no caffeine, no sugar." He drank.

"We saw the high winds on the news this morning," my mother put in. "We could really feel it in the car." She bustled past Ken and began pulling things out of the refrigerator. She held up a loaf of bread to me with a ginger, inviting smile.

"Good," I said, a little confused by all the commotion. "I'm starving."

My father reappeared in the doorway, expectantly lifting himself up on his toes and dropping down again, rustling his keys. Ken said abruptly that he had better go sit down. "OK," I almost shouted. He was fully dressed, at least—I had expected a flannel bathrobe—though his plaid shirt hung a little loosely. My father stepped aside for him to pass.

"Is there a tree?" I called after him, wishing for some sign that this would be a normal Christmas.

"A little one," he said, not turning.

"Oh, I want to go see!" I cried, pushing past my father to the living room.

A STRAINED yet cheerful activity pervaded the trim little house. My parents had systems of where to put groceries, what to prepare for each meal, when to do the laundry. It was surprisingly cold in San Diego, and that afternoon the windows of the house were steamy and festive. If I looked at Ken the right way, I could almost ignore the hollow quality in his eyes that ruthlessly identified him with every other AIDS patient.

When he wasn't aware of it, I watched that face carefully, looking for something deeper—some outward sign of how he was approaching his illness, what stance he now took toward the world. I couldn't imagine it. Was he resigned? Fierce? Frightened? On the other hand, how should he react? What would be the best approach to take?

Shortly before he went into the hospital, Ken had said to me on the phone, "It could hit me anytime. I can't worry about it." His voice was a little wild that day. "A guy I knew at work, he was walking down the street and, boom, he just collapsed. Blood clot. He was twenty-eight. So it can happen to anyone. I'm no different."

"That's true," I had murmured, distractedly scanning the contours of my shabby apartment, as if for some clue to what else might help him at this moment—the corrective analogy, the illuminating and soothing metaphor.

Now, too, I joined Ken in the complex rigors of positive thinking. He was eager to get back to work and begin living normally again, which I approved of heartily. The kitchen was filled with vitamins and organic food; in the freezer were yellowish ice-cube trays of something called AL-721. A pile of shiny paperbacks on health and healing overflowed the living-room mantel.

"I feel better now than I did before the pneumonia," Ken said, tapping his chest. "I was feeling worse and worse this fall, but now . . . "

I looked up from my sandwich. "Maybe you worked something out of your system," I suggested, offering the same amateur and whimsical logic that I might apply to a cold or stomach flu.

He shrugged, as if only just the right comforting explanation would do. "Maybe . . . "

3.

When did I first hear the story of my grandmother? Somewhere in the lost corridors of childhood—the time of walking under my mother's desk, the piano, past brown furniture legs; of loitering around the dining-room table, peering over the edge, from below the surface of adulthood—as my mother talked to a neighbor, a confidante. It was an adult story, one I only overheard, or was allowed to overhear. Not resting in my mother's arms—my ear to her chest, her voice there—but later, clinging to her hip perhaps as she sat over coffee.

Down there, barely comprehending, nevertheless I savored the pungent reality, finding its sourness almost pleasant: my grandmother could have been saved. But though it was a story about what might have been, it was told so many times that it became as inevitable as a melody, a nursery rhyme.

The legs of the dining-room table are strange. they don't come straight down from the four corners, but rather they start at the center of the table and curve outward onto the floor, like paws, and the square ends are brass-capped. The table used to be whitish bleached deco oak, but my grandfather stained it dark—"Mediterranean style"—on the one visit he made to California before he died. Ken and my mother helped—carefully staining, varnishing, rubbing the surface with steel wool between coats. It was a good visit, my mother liked to say. It was nice that her father had had something to do while he was there.

I've never asked, hearing the story of the forbidden cake, "What did Grandpa do?" At first, because I was a child and afraid to ask questions; more recently, because I feared the answer would upset my mother. In her version, my grandfather is the one who cares for my sick grandmother and then takes her to the hospital. But could he have simply stood by as she ate what wasn't good for her? Or later, week after week, as her health continued to worsen, the pain in her legs returned, and she finally lost consciousness and died? According to my Aunt Helen, not only did my grandfather do nothing to stop it, but he agreed with his wife completely. He and my grandmother were, it seems, equal partners in this death.

At night, before bed, he would leave chocolates for her on her pillow. "Go ahead," he would say. "These can't hurt you."

AROUND the dining-room table, every night after work, incompetence was my mother's favorite topic. Neal's, the decrepit downtown wig and beauty shop where she was the bookkeeper, seemed to offer infinite possibilities. Once my mother called a customer to tell her a check had bounced. "The poor lady couldn't understand why she didn't have any money in her account," my mother exclaimed. "She said, 'I still had checks left.'"

Stories of such utter stupidity were like nuggets of gold to my mother. She relished imitating these foolish voices, the bitter, inadvertent comedians of her world. The wig shop's owners, Neal and his wife, Reenie, were idiots! "You'll never guess what Reenie said to me today," my mother would begin, and the stories rolled out then, one after another, like uniformed messengers confirming over and over what my mother already knew about life.

Often there were tales of finding the single penny that would balance the books at last. My mother thought of herself as a detective, making sense of hopeless record keeping, sifting through the errors of Reenie and the staff. "Beauty operators . . . ledger . . . petty cash . . . " Terms I barely understood, or didn't know at all, rose and fell, repeated musically in each narrative. "It turned out she had forgotten to . . . " "He had crossed it out . . . " "Even after I . . . " "They had somehow . . . "

Early on, when the job and the stories were still new, my ten-year-old self must have struggled with the concept of problem solving. I may have piped up, "Why don't you tell them?"

My mother would have made a grunting, dismissive noise. "I tell them over and over. It doesn't do any darn good."

And my father would shake his head in agreement.

"Why don't you quit?" I may have persisted, but she wouldn't have answered. A child, I had said the wrong thing.

It would be years before I understood. Even in a world of idiots, my mother was often a timid participant. But I liked to think that whenever she backed down, my mother simply withheld her power, wisely, and that this too was a sign of her strong will. If she chose, the child in me believed, she could simply take over the world.

One year at the Christmas party the beauty operators put gin in the Coke machine. "That's dangerous!" my mother declared. It was her most disgusted and outraged voice, but even at eleven I half wondered why the beauty operators couldn't have a little fun once in a while. "Now, *what* if someone was on *antibiotics?*" my mother cried. "They could've had a *reaction.*" She emphasized the last word, technical and serious sounding, and the familiar smell of near tragedy hung over the dinner table like burned rubber—the burden of impending disaster, but also a queasy satisfaction, that of prediction, of having known the right answer all along.

But one of the beauty operators had said to her, "Ruth, do you take your clothes off when you take a shower?"

"*Ha, ha,*" my mother said to us, glaring, turning again to her potatoes with a child's defiance. "Hardy-har-har." I wasn't sure I understood the insult, but she seemed to have lost her normal glow for a moment, and I was sorry. I wanted her to win. And, after only a few bites, she was going again, her eyes bright and intent as usual, surveying with renewed assurance the week's sorry harvest of mistakes and negligence.

KEN KICKED ME under the table. I looked up and saw his half-suppressed shit-eating grin above the plastic flowers of the centerpiece, his tongue poking the side of his cheek. I had to look down at my plate so I wouldn't laugh. He had predicted it again: Neal's would take up the entire conversation.

When did that ritual begin? Perhaps it was the spring that Ken himself had gone to work at Neal's, after school as a stock boy. (It was 1969. There were a lot of wigs.) When he got home each night, he couldn't stand to hear about the place. "Sometimes I think I'll scream!" he'd whisper to me, back in his room.

I probably would not, on my own, have named my dinnertime boredom. But with Ken I teetered delightfully on the edge of a new subversion. I was only just learning that I, too, could play this kind of game. Often my mother would complain to Ken about my father, but I was rarely included in such conversations. Loitering nearby, I watched my mother's fitful face, and then Ken's, as he nodded gravely or offered a suggestion, understanding what I couldn't. My father—even if I had wanted to side with him instead—was usually traveling, or at work, or busy in the garage with boring automobile repairs.

I had also recently learned something else about conspiracy. One Saturday afternoon, I crept back down the hall to the kitchen, to overhear Ken and my mother talking. I had just argued with my brother and run to my room crying bitterly. Perhaps I returned to find out what I had known all along. Behind the pinkish, speckled wall, I heard my mother sigh in disgust and whisper, "He's too sensitive. He just can't take criticism . . . "

But now I was old enough for someone to whisper to me instead. Each night at dinner Mom would begin, "Oh, that Reenie . . . " and I'd feel Ken's toe on my sock, electric and sensual. With each successive story he'd search for my foot, between the square paws of the table, and nudge me. I knew

muppet plays and the drawing of cartoons would follow immediately in my room after dinner. If I paid no attention, fearing my
mother might notice, he'd kick me harder until I had to look up.

AFTER KEN went away to college, the number of possible group-
ings diminished, and the house was stricken with a desperate
boredom. It was just me against my mother and my father, and I
now had no one to turn to. Or, more to my liking but still
painfully incomplete, it was just me and my mother against my
father.

Sighing and tisking, she sat at the dining-room table with a
sharp scissors undoing the stitches on my father's pants. She
shook the little pieces of thread from the seam and began picking at it again. "*He* gains weight, and then *I* have to let out the
waist."

Probably my father was out of town on business, and I was
waiting for dinner to finish cooking. In the kitchen, steam
would be rising under the single stove light. I watched as my
mother worked away some more, and soon the seam was un-
done. She shook out the pants again and reached for the pins
and her little ruler.

"One time he came to me and asked me to let out the waist a
half inch." She rolled her eyes. "Well, that was when my *father*
was visiting." She pronounced "my father" as if here were a figure that could melt all injustice and stupidity. "He said to Dad,
'Dave, that's only a quarter-inch seam.' My father was almost
eighty-five then, but he was still pretty sharp."

I followed her as she took the pinned pants into the bedroom and sat at her sewing machine. I settled on the padded

clothes hamper. The Singer whirred, and my mother resumed: "Dad used to say to my father, 'She's a real lemon. I want my money back.' And my father would say, not even cracking a smile, 'Anytime you want to give her back, Dave, we'd be glad to have her. Anytime.'"

I rocked on my hands, as if kneading my mother's growing outrage into the bread of revolution. In seventh grade I myself was learning a lot about ignominy.... But already she was done. She pulled the two threads out from the machine and deftly clipped. Then she went to check on dinner.

We would eat together in the family room, just the two of us, watching a rerun of *Star Trek*. "Dad's not around," my mother would whisper, meaning that instead of setting the table, I could put up the TV trays. My father hated *Star Trek*. My mother made it clear, however, that she didn't mind at all granting me this treat of tight clothing on distant planets. Later *The Courtship of Eddie's Father* came on, a program about a single parent and his cute son, and my mother would grow extra-affectionate. "You're my only child left," she would tell me.

My mother worked hard to win my love at such times, drawing me into her glowing circle of camaraderie. Requests my father was sure to veto were granted—wire-frame glasses, a stereo of my own—and I had only to hope that my mother could somehow follow through and persuade my father before he said no once and for all.

Just as I had previously wondered why my mother didn't quit her job, I began now to think she should divorce my father. There were so many things about her that he didn't understand—her music, for instance. My own quarrels with him were more and more frequent, sometimes over the smallest things—a light left on, a glass without a coaster. During the news he barked at the TV: "Just look at those jigaboos . . . " "If it was up to me, we would have blown up Vietnam a long time ago . . . " "Hitler knew how to run a country . . . " I was old enough to have my own views, but each argument we had was more futile than the last, and my father's wrath turned from the TV to me. Life was simply easier when he was away on business.

Each of my mother's confidences fed my new sense of injustice. I took her idle complaints with the utmost gravity, as if our conversations were consciousness-raising sessions in our own civil-rights movement. "I'll never forget that winter in Wheaton," she'd say, "when the pipes froze, and Dad was traveling—of course. He always missed every single crisis that way, and I was left holding the bag. That house in Wheaton was one thing after another."

"I remember the basement flooding," I'd offer.

She nodded with exaggerated knowing, her lips pursed. Perhaps it was Saturday and she was baking cookies, placing the last loaded pan in the oven. She offered me the big yellow bowl to lick, the leavings of raw, sweet, indigestible dough.

"It took me six months to sell that house before we could move to Louisiana," she said. "No one wanted it."

Licking my finger, I recalled this distant time when my father was almost entirely absent, working in New Orleans before the rest of the family could join him. I remembered wondering, one day when I was about four, who was this strange man making popcorn in my mother's kitchen?

"And before he got that job, he was out of work almost a year. Both the girls were in college, and we had to go into savings." She began washing her baking utensils with a certain vengeance. "I had to teach myself shorthand, so I could go to Kelly Girls in Chicago."

And I imagined my plucky mother riding on the train into the city, eking out a living during hard times—like the stories of her childhood and the Depression she also liked to tell. "I don't know how we got through it," she'd always sigh, and I'd silently agree that it must have been no thanks to my father.

I SAT AS USUAL on the clothes hamper, watching her brush out her hair. She had just taken off her wig and placed it on the faceless Styrofoam.

"He's been so upset about work, he's gone and given himself a *rash!*" she was saying.

"What's he so upset about?" I asked. We never needed to use my father's name.

"Oh, he's afraid he won't get this project done on time. Yes, it's a terrible deadline, but he just lets it get to him! He can't sleep. He's tossing and turning, and then *I* can't sleep." She began nervously zipping her wig into its vinyl case. "I don't let work do that to me. I just don't."

I nodded. She resumed brushing her hair.

"So he woke up with this rash yesterday morning. All across his chest and face"—her voice dropped to a whisper—"and up and down his legs, too." She gestured with the brush. "I told him it was just nerves, but he wouldn't listen to me, of course.

So yesterday afternoon he went to the *doctor.*" She raised one eyebrow, then she opened the little drawer next to the sink. "And he gave him these—for the 'rash.'" She held up the brownish orange plastic vial. "Dad didn't even look at the label, and Doctor Michael was probably hoping he wouldn't. But I know what they are." She shook the vial, and the pills rattled like a fine rain. "These aren't for a rash at all," she declared. "They're *tranquilizers.*"

4.

I carried the last plate into the little dining room, putting off just a moment longer sitting down with Ken and my parents. Warily I joined the circle under the hanging light, wondering if the tone of honesty Ken had described would continue. I was relieved and disappointed to find that the family had reverted to small talk. Everything seemed both boring and reassuringly normal. My mother had made her midwestern chili, the meal we always had on Christmas Eve.

After supper, as soon as the dishes were done, my parents prepared to leave for the hotel. Only I was staying at the house with Ken, a privilege I had anticipated for weeks now. Hearing my parents' car chug away in the cold, I turned to Ken in my stocking feet with something of the elation of childhood. For a second it seemed like we were kids again, on our own for the night.

We sat down on the couch, just the two of us. His living room seemed small and cozy, the short tree blinking in the corner. "I remember one time lying under the tree in San Jose, with our glasses off," I said. "And the lights looked so big, with big halos."

Ken didn't say anything, and I realized that this scene, so vivid to me all these years, perhaps wasn't even a memory for him.

"So, you're doing OK," I said. "You seem pretty good."

He nodded, and there was a long silence. I had been waiting all day for this moment, but now I didn't know what to say.

"Should we see what's on TV?" Ken suggested. I was disappointed. He opened the listings. "I guess there's nothing really on until nine." He continued paging through, looking distracted.

"Ken," I said. He put the guide down, and I blurted, "Why didn't you call anyone when you went into the hospital?"

He smoothed the nubby cushion with one hand. "I thought I was going to die," he replied. "There didn't seem to be any point. . . . I really didn't think I was going to make it."

I nodded, though I didn't understand in the least. Did he want to be alone if he was going to die? Why wouldn't he at least have contacted me, who already knew he was sick? Was there some reason he didn't feel he could trust me?

"Then you called Mom and Dad," I said.

"By then I was getting better."

"Yeah . . . " I was perplexed. Maybe I would understand later. "It's just that it was—strange that no one called me. I had no idea. And then *I* tried to call *you* that day, and Mom answers and tells me . . . It was just strange," I repeated.

"We didn't call anyone," he said. "There really wasn't time."

I nodded vaguely. This was exactly what my mother had told me.

HE WENT into the bathroom to take out his contact lenses. I noted on his bookshelf the spine of a literary journal I had sent him the year before because it contained a short story of mine. I wondered if he had liked it. He returned wearing his old black glasses, looking awkward and pale.

"You look like Clark Kent," I said.

"I know. That's why I never wear these." He stood before me purposefully. "There's something I need to talk to you about."

I nodded, pulling my feet up under me on the couch, grateful for this sign of trust. He sat down beside me, staring ahead in concentration.

"I've been thinking about changing my will," he began.

I nearly shut my eyes and plugged my ears. I didn't want to hear anything having to do with his death. "Do we have to talk about this?" I was hugging myself and rocking back and forth.

"I really think we should," he said. "But we could wait if you want . . ."

His voice fell off. Neither did I want to disappoint him in any way, if possible. I stopped myself rocking but kept my arms wrapped around myself. I noticed how cold the house was. "Brr," I murmured. "All right."

He cleared his throat. He began speaking quickly and without emotion. "So right now it says that if Mom and Dad aren't alive when I die, then my estate will be divided between all four siblings."

I muttered assent, trying to play along. But then, without warning, he said something very strange: "I've decided I should cut everyone else out."

I blinked, trying to understand. His eyes were a little unsteady behind those thick glasses. "You mean—you wouldn't include Carol, Janet, and Paul?" I asked.

"Yes, so you'd be sole heir," he said efficiently. "That is, if Mom and Dad aren't alive when I die." His nervous hands patted the air. "If they are alive, everything would go to them. So this is all just hypothetical."

I nodded. "Hypothetical." Scenarios and dollar signs danced before me. For a moment the idea of a large sum of money was divorced from all context, and I saw myself buying an apartment, quitting my job, taking a year off to write . . .

"But why?" I asked, trying to shake myself free of my own imagination.

"I'm not as close to the others," he said. "And they don't need the money."

I felt a bizarre yet somehow familiar spotlight shining on me. Something told me I must extricate myself at all costs. "None of us needs the money," I replied. "I don't need the money either, no more than anyone else." I searched frantically for arguments. "Carol isn't that much better off than I am. And Janet has been in debt . . . "

Ken frowned. "I thought that you needed more time to write. You're always saying that. And that you're always struggling for money."

"I can take care of myself," I said. "Don't worry about me."

He pondered for a moment. Exactly what I was trying to extricate myself from, I'm not sure. I doubted there were no strings to this offer. Once, a few months before, Ken had asked me if I might move to San Diego if he got really sick. Was that the kind of thing we were really talking about now? Or was he asking for something more ineffable and, therefore, more profound? Perhaps he was asking me to agree to see the world the way he saw it, or wanted to see it—a world where someone is always left out.

It was a tendency I had lately come to hate in myself.

But Ken's face looked worried and gaunt, lost in thought. How could I be on his side, but not only his side?

"I could include Carol and Janet," he said at last. "But not Paul."

I knit my brow. Rather than escape, it seemed I had only dug myself deeper. "Why—why not Paul?" I stammered.

Ken's mouth compressed, and quickly he appeared lost in a maze of his own troubles. "First of all, he definitely doesn't need the money. He's better off than anyone else." I said nothing, but Ken must have seen that I felt this was no argument. "Secondly, Cynthia doesn't like me." He was referring to Paul's wife, with whom he had had a big fight a few years back, thinly patched over. "We've never gotten along. And the last time they were in San Diego, they called me once, and they said they didn't have time to get together. They were here for a whole week, on vacation, ten miles up the coast."

On an earlier occasion, I might have just taken Ken's side,

which would have been simpler. But tonight I wanted to take a stand against conspiracy. I would remain absolutely neutral. "I can see that, but . . . " I tried to think of something convincing to say. "Do you really want to leave behind that kind of final statement?"

He didn't seem to hear me. "I still have a lot of resentment toward him. About childhood."

Though I knew how much Ken and Paul fought as kids, this was the first I had heard of a grudge.

"I spent a lot of time talking about it, back when I was in therapy," Ken said. "Paul teased me all the time when I was little. All the time. He and his damn friends." He grimaced. "I have a lot of really bad memories."

I remembered one story. "It's Saturday," Paul and his friend Robbie used to tell Ken, every Monday.

"No, it isn't," the six-year-old would say.

"Saturday! Saturday!" they'd yell, over and over and over, until Ken ran off crying.

And I recalled the things Ken had, in turn, done to me when I was a kid—the teasing, the sarcasm, the frequent socks on the arm—and I wondered about the family, how all of this was allowed to go on, so much that it could mire Ken in rancor even now. As for my own torments, Ken had asked me about them on at least one occasion, but I didn't want to think about that now, of all times. What did it matter? I just wanted him to get well. And yet I also wanted to shout, "Can't you just forget about what Paul did to you and get on with it?"

I searched for some appropriate formulation. "You're going to need everyone's help in your—recovery." I spoke the last word as if that were indeed possible—whether for his sake or mine, I'm not sure. "You'll need everyone on your side," I said carefully. "So I think you should include everyone in your will."

For an instant I was proud of this logical turn, as if I had found the right words to close the chapter. But Ken sat musing and red-faced still, pressing his long, square fingers together to make a tense little house.

KEN WAS LONG asleep. Like a sorcerer in the night, I went to his mantel and examined the colorful pile of healing books. Friends had given them to him in the hospital. "Overkill," Ken had said wryly. But he had started reading them.

You Can Heal Your Life said the one on top. I picked it up.

Resentment that is long held can eat away at the body and become the disease we call cancer. Criticism as a permanent habit can often lead to arthritis in the body. Guilt always looks for punishment, and punishment creates pain. . . .

The book had a heart-shaped rainbow on the cover and was cheaply printed. *"New York Times* Best Seller," it said. Feeling unaccountably weary, I flipped ahead.

Interestingly, migraine headaches can almost always be alleviated by masturbation. . . .

Whenever I see small children wearing glasses, I know there is stuff going on in their household they do not want to look at.

I glanced up. Here in Ken's house in San Diego, it seemed, the family had come full circle. But I couldn't yet stop paging through, mesmerized by this old, murky whirlpool.

The innermost belief for everyone I have worked with is always, "I'm not good enough! . . ."

It is my belief that VENEREAL DISEASE is almost always sexual guilt. . . .

. . . for many gay men the experience of getting old is something to dread. It is almost better to die than to get old. And AIDS is a disease that often kills.

In a gesture of exaggerated disgust, as if someone were watching me, I threw the book down. I glanced helplessly around the dark, empty living room. I wanted somehow to expunge this influence from the house and Ken's life. Seeking other, better omens, I picked up another volume.

She made sure she was in control of the situation and ready for every eventuality. She is alive and well today. . . .

Since then, he has practically made a career of exercise. . . . Seven years later he is free of disease.

The "M.D." after the author's name reassured me. *Love, Medicine and Miracles*, the book was called. Perhaps there really was something here that might offer Ken hope. I took it over to the couch, got under the blanket, and began reading with dizzy intensity. The uplifting stories reeled out, one after another, like flute notes up the same uneven scale.

In a few months Bruce's liver tests were normal, he conquered his other problems, and required no surgery. . . .

He was able to complete his course of therapy with no further problems, and he is well today. . . .

Then one day in the group she asked, "Who knows when I received my chemotherapy?" No one did. "I got it forty-five minutes ago," she exulted, "and here I am feeling fine."—

I heard Ken stir in the next room. As if I had been caught masturbating, I quickly put down the book, shut out the light, and closed my eyes.

THE NEXT MORNING I watched Ken put his wallet and change into his pocket. Mom and Dad would be here soon. Our conversation of the night before seemed to have been forgotten, and he was in a good mood. It was Christmas morning.

He held up a pair of socks to me. "Is white OK?"

I nodded eagerly.

I saw that in his top bureau drawer, next to the condoms, lay his oldest puppets. They predated the muppets and were never my toys. But I took them out, the tiger and the dog. They still had very nice fur.

"Hello, Ken," I said in a high voice, gesturing with the puppets' arms. "How are you?"

Deeper in the drawer were his two stuffed dogs. "Ah, yes," Ken said, taking the dogs out. I lay the puppets aside. "Tiger and Ruff were nice, but Mama-Dog and Puppy-Dog were my real friends," he said. They were basset shaped, one larger than the other, faded brown terry cloth worn smooth, their closed, black-felt eyelashes nearly gone. He set them out on the dresser.

"We left them behind at a motel once," Ken said. "We had been driving maybe an hour when I noticed. I was, what, four. Mom says Dad didn't want to turn back for them, but I cried and cried."

I picked them both up and hugged them. They were worth going back for, I thought.

THAT AFTERNOON, when the presents had been opened, the four of us went for a drive along the shore. I thought, Here's the rocky coast I saw from the plane. The narrow road wound along cliffs that dropped steeply to the water.

"This is a real Jimmy Olson road," I said, poking Ken on the shoulder. It was what he and I called all windy roads—the repeated location in every third *Superman* episode, where the boy reporter's brakes go and Superman has to come stop the car just before it goes over the edge.

I was hoping we'd find a secluded spot to walk along the water, but the road only circled back, and apparently there was no park here. We ended up at a suburban beach Ken used to go to all the time, back when he was in graduate school here, when he had a girlfriend. There were houses and stores all along the edge. I was disappointed: I wanted something more untouched.

We plodded to the far end, sat down on the rocks for a little while, a dirt cliff behind us. Ken seemed glum under the brim of his hat, the glow of Christmas gone.

I asked my mother if she wanted to walk some more. Ken and my father stayed behind. This was the first time on this visit that my mother and I had been alone, and I noted to myself that she had not once complained about my father. My brother was her only concern now.

"I remember that time when Ken was just five, and he ran off to the dime store by himself," she said, staring down at the sand. "No one knew where he'd gone. I thought I'd go out of my mind!"

"I think I remember that story," I murmured. She sounded very sad and far away. I tried to imagine what it must be like, to have nearly lost Ken, her son, and to be losing him yet. But I couldn't quite trick my mind into distance. I myself had nearly lost my brother, and I wished I could get comfort now from my mother.

"That afternoon I went to the market, and I told Janet and Paul to keep an eye on Ken. 'Oh, sure,' they said." My mother grimaced and nodded, rolling her eyes. "So Ken decides he wants to go to the five-and-dime, and he tells Janet and Paul—and they didn't pay any attention to him. They were probably watching TV.

"So he puts on his little red jacket all by himself and he goes to the store. It was about a mile down the Post Road."

Suddenly I felt I could hardly bear the weight of this story, whose meaning my mother would never herself fully articulate.

"So then I get home from the market, and I don't see him anywhere. 'Where's Ken?' I ask them. 'I dunno.' " She pulled a face again. "Well, I looked out in the yard, and then I started looking up and down the block. I asked the neighbors—nobody had seen him."

We had stopped walking and stood facing the sea. I began myself to feel invisible, unaccounted for.

It seemed I knew too much, and what was I going to do with that knowledge? And yet I also wanted to let her have the memory in its simplicity and fullness, and whatever its telling might accomplish for her at this moment. "Reel her out," I said to myself. I imagined letting her go way out, a fish at play, far into the even rows of waves before me.

"By this time I was practically tearing my hair out," she said, pretending to pull on her hair, making a comical grunting sound. "I was just about to call the police when I heard a knock at the front door. It was one of the neighbors, from down the block. 'Excuse me,' she said, very timidly, 'but I think I saw your little boy walking along the Post Road just now. I asked him if he wanted a ride home, but he said he wasn't allowed to talk to strangers.'"

My mother shrugged and chuckled in an exasperated way. "I was about to get in the car when the police drove up. There was Ken sitting in the front seat, between the two officers."

We had turned back down the beach and were about halfway to Ken and my father now, who were huddled on the rocks, hands in their pockets. To our right, the waves continued rolling forward in straight lines one after the other, like obedient soldiers, and then slipping away again.

"The policemen said Ken hadn't wanted any help from them either," she said. "I can just see him there, very independent, in his little red jacket, five years old, walking along the Post Road. He knew exactly where he was going. He had been to the store, and now he was on his way home."

I grunted acknowledgment, and we walked in silence. I looked at Ken, a distant figure still—the lost boy. "Home"—did that mean health, or death? I began playing a mental game, as if the future depended on my interpretation. But it could only mean death, and that my mother was already letting go. I tried to erase that version, tried to make "home" equal "health." Ken had to find his own way, yes, but it would be the way toward continued health. That was what I wanted this story to mean in the end.

My mother chuckled once more. Her story wasn't over. "The cops said that when they pulled up beside him on the road, Ken just kept walking, ignoring them. One of them called out, 'Hey, Bud, what are you doing there?'" My mother cocked her chin saucily. "And Ken shot back, not even turning his head, 'My name isn't Bud.'"

Normal Heights

A JAMAICAN CAB DRIVER once told me a story:
"I was riding in a truck with my good friend," he said. "We were on our way to Kingston, and my friend was driving. The roads were very narrow, very narrow, and windy, with no shoulder and just room for two cars to pass one another, and a ditch. This was in the mountains.

"So, we came around a bend onto the straightaway, and there was another truck coming in the other direction, and then we saw a motorcycle, a little motorcycle, come out from behind the truck to pass. Motorcycle was headed straight toward us." The cab driver gestured with his hand above the steering wheel. "There was our truck, and the other truck, and then the motor- cycle, and there was no room.

"My friend, he turns to me and says, 'Shall I save his life?'

"And very quick, he turns the wheel, and just like that, he puts the truck in the ditch. Right in the ditch. And the motorcycle zooms past, just between us and the other truck—shoo!" The cab driver gestured again with his hand.

"So my friend's truck, it's on its side in the ditch, and we're sitting there a minute, you know, trying to catch our breath. We hear the motorcycle coming back again. Motorcycle drives up to the window to see if we're all right. My good friend, he turns to look at the man—

"It was his brother."

2.

The August weekend slowly wheeling through Sunday evening and breaking apart, Ken called. I lay back under the ceiling fan in the heat. "How are you?" I asked.

"Depressed," he murmured. "I just made dinner. The kitchen's a mess. I just don't feel like cleaning it up."

It was muggy, and like nearly every Sunday night, I felt the weight of the workweek like an impending jail sentence. Maybe I would call in sick the following morning. "How are you feeling—physically?"

"OK," he said defensively.

This was about eight months after his first bout with pneumonia. The hope inspired by somehow living through that crisis had long worn off.

There was a long, dead pause. I tried to think of something to say. "How was your weekend?"

"OK."

Silence again. This had been going on for weeks now. I heard him breathing on the line. Each time he called it was as if he had started the car and then turned to me, gesturing forward, urgently and in no particular direction, gesturing, "Well? Well?"

I said, "I'm looking forward to our train trip next month."

"Yeah."

We had been planning this trip, from San Jose to San Diego, ever since last Christmas, after he was so sick. But tonight the idea didn't seem to budge him. "So, what's going on?"

"Nothing . . ." Something in his tone made my heart quicken. Perhaps I didn't want to know. He sighed, and then even the spark of irritation left his voice. "Sometimes I just don't know if I can go on."

Startled, I let more silence surround such a sudden, naked moment. I sat up on the bed and stared out the black bedroom window. I had never grown accustomed to it, this changing places, my older brother in need.

But once again he had chosen me to confide in. There had to be some kind of answer. "Have you thought more about going back into therapy?" I tried.

"Not really."

I remember now a childhood joke between Ken and me: we used to write Dear Abby columns in which no matter what the letter was, no matter how simple the problem or how long and involved, Abby replied, "See a counselor."

"The guy I was seeing before is useless," he muttered.

From the threads of boredom, disappointment, and fear, I tried to weave a response. "Well, it's certainly true there are lots of really bad shrinks around," I said very objectively. "This other guy didn't help you?"

"No—and I'm not going on antidepressants either." A friend had recently suggested this to him, and he had told me how much it had annoyed him.

"All right, all right." I waited a moment, but I was determined to persist this one time. "Maybe you could find a better therapist?"

"I can always go to a meeting," he said. "I go two or three nights a week."

He meant Narcotics Anonymous. Though I believed in therapy, I had little faith at the time in Twelve Step programs. Looking back, my preferences seem completely arbitrary, as if I may as well have been advocating transcendental meditation, or yoga, or Christian Science as the answer.

"That's a lot of meetings," I replied.

"Mm."

I wanted to shout, "It isn't helping you! Don't you see? Why don't you do something!"

"What about a support group?" I offered.

"Maybe *you* should join a support group."

I stared at the ceiling, twisting the phone cord around my hand. "You mean for people close to someone with AIDS," I said cagily. "Well, I may look into it."

Ken explained that he had tried the local group for HIV-positive men. "It was just a bunch of fags sitting around bitching about their medication," he said. "I got really sick of it."

I had to admit that I could understand that, and we were at another impasse. "But, a good shrink—"

"Cliff, I see too many doctors already! I have appointments three, four times a week as it is. I'm sick of it."

Here were the blank and hopeless realities of terminal illness that I couldn't even imagine. I didn't want to talk about doctors. "I can understand that," I said, "but—"

"Can we just drop it?"

His voice had taken on that final quality of seething annoyance I'd known since childhood—the family voice of ultimate panic and warning. An ancient timidity rose in me. Angry with it, I pushed blindly ahead. Was I pursuing at last a new and brilliant course of honesty and action, contrary to years of stoic, soul-destroying denial? Or did I only want to be like a television character, one who speaks his mind and confronts those around him just at the right moment, bringing about spectacular resolutions to seemingly intractable problems, all in a matter of minutes?

"I just think it would be good for you to have someone to talk to," I persisted. "There, in San Diego, I mean." This I added hastily to say that of course I didn't mean he couldn't also talk to me. He didn't reply, and his silence bloomed into accusation—all that I couldn't or wouldn't do for him, now or ever. My tone grew theoretical. "It's just that when someone keeps saying they're down, one is bound to suggest something—"

"Therapy isn't going to make any goddamn difference," he said. And then his final arrow hit its mark. "Of course I'm depressed. I'm dying. No—I'm *happy* to be dying of a hideous, incurable disease."

Even now, five years later, I want to stop and turn to the jury and say, "See? See what I was up against?" And still I want to be the hero of the story—of a simple story, in which I offer the right answer and it's rejected. And yet I also find myself thinking now, "Good, Ken. You tell him." Because his anger, even his bitterness, shows me a spark of life—his life.

I sighed, furious, resigned to changing the subject. The long-distance line whooshed softly.

3.

"I need to talk to you about childhood," Ken said. This was the previous summer, part of the acceleration of friendship and late-night phone conversations that led up to his illness. "My sponsor says that I need to make amends."

"I've heard about that," I said. My last boyfriend was in AA.

He paused. "Is there anything from childhood that I did that you remember as hurtful?"

It sounded like a prepared speech. "Hmm," I said suspiciously. In fact, the ex-boyfriend in AA was still at the top of my jerk list, and I had been skeptical of the Program ever since. I thought of Pat Heaney, the only other person I knew in AA, and his calling up his high school drama teacher quite recently and telling him, "I'm sorry I hated you all these years."

I said, "I would think you have things you're angry at *me* about."

"Not really," Ken replied.

I said that I couldn't really think of anything either. "I mean, we were just kids . . . " Though actually I was beginning to warm to the subject. I looked up at the ceiling, which was pebbly and white. Was there a way to talk about childhood—I mean, really talk about it?

"Yeah, it was all just kid kind of stuff," Ken quickly agreed. "That's what I told my sponsor. But she keeps hassling me about it."

"Huh . . . " I began pulling at the tangles in the curly phone cord. "I'm not sure I get this business of making amends," I said.

Ken said he didn't really understand it either.

4.

"So many people close to me are sick," said my sister Carol. "It's really upsetting."

We were eating lunch the day Ken was to arrive in San Jose. My parents did not respond. The meal continued, forks scraping. Since Ken's last recovery, they wouldn't talk about his illness. Breezily my mother began telling a story about someone at church who was very old and surprisingly spry. I had to admire Carol's temerity. Perhaps because she is the oldest, or because she had just arrived from France, she seemed out of touch with the family rules.

I remembered something my shrink said to me before I left for California: "The boat is already rocking." Earlier in the day, as I sat down to breakfast, I saw it, almost hallucinated it. I looked at my mother and father as they talked of the next-door neighbor's having died of cancer. My mother told how the widow had said to her, "Life isn't fair." "No, it isn't," my mother had replied. "Life isn't fair." She shook her head, and I dared not make any explicit connections.

Neither could I speak up now. Across from me, Carol was eating quietly. We could talk later, I decided, not only about Ken, but about how frustrating this silence was, how oblivious Mom and Dad could be.

"Last night I dreamed I was doing magic tricks," my mother said suddenly. She turned to me. "And I saw you out in the audience. You came in and whispered to someone."

THAT AFTERNOON, waiting to go pick up Ken, I wandered forlornly from the kitchen into the family room, playing with a bottle, and sat down next to my mother on the couch. She was lying with her knees up, under the colorful old afghan, reading. Carol was in the living room asleep with jet lag, Dad out front wiping off his car. I listened to the sparrows out in the yard, peered through the sliding screen door at the tree full of oranges.

"I wish Ken weren't sick," I said childishly, staring down.

"So do I," she said quietly and went on reading. A swirling, knitting silence. Even if she asked me more, I wondered, what would I answer? Suddenly I grew completely blank, unable to see what I could possibly want from her at this moment.

In a little while I got up to put the empty bottle in the garage. My father was just folding up his special car-care cloth, which smelled like toothpaste. Light poured in from the street and around the two cars. He pressed the two buttons above his head and the garage door began to fold shut. No longer in silhouette, his face became clear under the fluorescents. He said, "Better hurry up and get ready."

At the airport, my mother and I left Carol and my father in the car and went to the gate. But the crowd of passengers quickly petered to nothing, and still we did not see Ken.

"The flight must have been early," my mother said uneasily. She stared at the empty primary colors of the airline desk. "He must have been one of the first ones off." But perhaps she, too, wondered if he had in fact missed the flight, too sick to travel after all. This was his first visit home since he got sick.

I left my mother and went out front to the car. In the twilight I saw two heads in back, Carol's and Ken's. Somehow he had slipped past. I went to the door to make sure, and he looked up to me through the window with the eyes of a sick and excited child.

5.

I'm hiding behind the beige chair. Ken is looking for me. "Where are you?" he calls out. "Where are you?"

I giggle, but he doesn't seem to hear. He comes nearer. He stands right next to me.

"Where are you?" he keeps saying, looking this way and that. "Come out, come out, wherever you are."

I reach out and touch his arm. "Here."

He turns. "I can't see you. You're invisible."

"I'm right here," I say. "You found me."

"I can't see you," he says. "You're invisible. I can't see you."

I look down at my own hands, trying to think how to make myself substantial again. "Stop it!" I say at last.

"Invisible! Invisible!" he sings.

I run out of the room.

KEN HOLDS both my wrists. He pushes my hand to my face. "Stop hitting yourself, Cliff." He's grinning ear to ear, his face pasty and wide. He pushes my other hand to my face. "Stop hitting yourself!"

"CLII-IFF."

I pretend to be engrossed in my homework.

"Clii-iff."

I look up at Ken standing in the doorway, rubbing his eye with his middle finger—Fuck You—rubbing and rubbing. "There's something in my eye, Cliff!" Rubbing with his middle finger and grinning at me. His glasses bob up and down on his nose. "There's something in my eye!"

"COME ON. Play." I hold up the old, black Monopoly box in dismay. I rattle it once. "Come on."

He lies on his bed in his room listening to *Sgt. Pepper's*.

"You're not doing anything," I say. "Come on."

He taps the wall with his foot. I try to think how I can get him to do what I want. "I'll go set up the game right now. In my room." It's an urgent mystery to me, what will tip the invisible scales of his boredom and make him reply, simply and without enthusiasm, "All right." I opt for a kind of casual pleading. "Come on. Why not?"

Suddenly he jumps up and switches off the record player. My eyes widen in possible hope. He says, "Let's not and say we did."

6.

"How's work, Ken?" asked my father jovially.

"OK." His voice had a slightly defensive tone all the time now. He passed the corn muffins. "Everyone there is such a ditz. I never should have taken a government job," he said, warming to the subject, a favorite of his, in an absentminded way. "They're all in semiretirement already."

My mother laughed too loudly.

"That's how it is with any job," my father declared. "If you want something done, and done right, you have to do it yourself."

There was a pause. What we all knew, and what could not be spoken, was that this family gathering would never have happened if Ken weren't sick. Normally I made it to California no more than once a year, for Christmas. Carol only occasionally made it even then. But here it was September, no occasion whatsoever, and here we all were, as if by some gay coincidence.

"You try to explain something to these people," Ken said. He shook his head in disgust.

"Wasting your time," my father answered. He was about to dip his spoon in the bowl, but we had all taken our cue from my mother and paused with our hands in our laps. My father shrugged and bowed his head.

My mother's voice was quavery. "Bless this food, and make us good. For Jesus' sake, Amen." It was the same prayer that Ken used to speak, and then me, and now it had passed back to my mother again. We all looked up nervously, as if from a shot at the doctor's.

Ken seemed dangerously flushed with his ambiguous, pivotal role as unspoken guest of honor. Not quite as gaunt as he was just after the pneumonia, nevertheless he appeared absorbed in his own, unarticulated poignancy. Shakily he raised a spoon of chili to his lips.

Carol said, "This is really good, Mom."

Ken and I both attempted hearty assents.

"Mother's food is always excellent," said my father, just as he has said a thousand times before.

"Sure is," Ken affirmed, as if to say that he would be around to agree another thousand times.

"Mm. Corn muffins," said Carol, reaching for another. "Yum, yum."

There was another pause, spongy and enervating, seeming to glow with the mute, damning conviction that each and every moment was some sort of last chance.

"How's your house, Ken?" boomed my father.

"Fine."

"Ken's house is really cute," I informed my sister. She hadn't come to San Diego the previous Christmas. "And the neighborhood is really nice too."

"Yeah," said Ken. "When I first moved to Normal Heights, it seemed really out of the way, but now it seems like everyone is moving there."

"I guess everyone found those heights more and more normal," said Carol, letting go her ready, high-pitched cackle. Ken chuckled too, and the old family hilarity seemed to be in swing for a moment. But I could think of no new pun to keep it going.

"There was a Normal, Illinois," my mother recalled. "Dad and I used to laugh at the signs near the school—'Please be careful of Normal children.'" Like most of my mother's jokes, this one fell a little flat. "Normal children," she repeated, shaking her head and smiling to herself.

7.

I watched Ken rooting in his suitcase distractedly.

"So, are we going to get our train tickets tomorrow?" I asked.

"Goddamn it." He didn't look up.

"What?"

"I forgot something . . . "

I wondered if it might be medicine. "Anything important?"

He half shook himself, and glanced at me with vague eyes. To the usual awkwardness of seeing one another barely once a year, we had now added our telephone disagreements over his illness. "Oh, the train. I'd rather fly down this time."

For months we had been talking about making this journey to San Diego by train. And yet neither was I very enthusiastic about it lately.

"A twelve-hour trip isn't a good idea right now, Cliffy. I just can't handle it right now."

I assented. But he appeared to have given up the idea too easily. It had never quite seemed to me that we had made up after that fight about therapy a few weeks before.

"I'll pay for your plane ticket down," he said with sudden geniality. He pulled several orange bottles of pills from his suitcase and put them aside on the bed. "I bought a round trip for myself. It was really cheap, so . . . "

I let this reassure me that he wasn't mad anymore, and he really did want to see me. I decided to let it go. "Great," I said. "That would be a big help."

So here we were, like so many visits before, alone in my old room together, at the very end of the house, away from everyone else. He got up and began nervously hanging up a couple of things. Settling into prime little-brother mode, I lingered, watching his every move, waiting for nothing in particular to happen.

I stretched out on my side, cupped my head in my hand. "So, how's everything?"

He seemed to twitch. He sat down across from me, stared at his feet. "Not too good, actually." He placed his hands together between his knees, wiggling them like the tail of a fish. "I've been really suicidal."

I barely shifted on the bed. "Really," I said, as if I weren't the least bit frightened. But this was the first time he had come right out and said it.

He straightened, grimaced a moment. "I don't know, maybe I *should* go on antidepressants."

I swallowed, fingering the bedspread. Years later I would understand that it wasn't exactly death that my brother was afraid of. It was living with his illness, the possibility of not being able to take care of himself, of losing his job and his insurance, of poverty, disability, disfigurement—and of giving up his faculties, which was, in fact, what happened in the end. I, on the other hand, was most afraid that he would die. I saw him quitting the fight already, slipping away from me grain by grain. And I wanted to shout, "Don't die. Just don't die."

I said, "Do you think that would help?"

He replied that his friend Jeff said antidepressants had helped him. "But . . . " He waved his hand. "Pills, pills, pills."

"Yeah," I breathed. I tried to sound sympathetic. But we had arrived once more in the eggshell territory of our running argument.

"Listen, I'm really tired," he said, sounding annoyed. It couldn't have been 8:30. "I'm gonna go to sleep."

I replied as if this were perfectly natural. "You've been working all week, huh?"

He didn't nod. Again an expression of physical pain crossed his gaunt, reddened face, and was gone.

"OK, good night," I said cheerfully, getting up. I shut the door quietly, stood in the hallway a moment looking at the sliver of yellow light leaking out.

ALL EVENING the still-new disease came up on TV. Public-service announcements, news reports, upcoming dramas. The nation seemed to have followed us into our new neighborhood of horror and grief, and like an eager newcomer, it had its own brightly colored ideas about how to comprehend, how to settle into the unfamiliar landscape. To me, the word *AIDS* seemed to boom out of the TV set. From the La-Z-Boy I would glance sidewise at my parents and my sister seated in a row on the couch, staring at the screen, munching popcorn.

Later, after eleven, I crept back down the hall to Ken. The thin door gave way with a squeak, and a wall of hot air hit me. This room was usually the coldest in the house. But Ken must have turned the space heater to high, and with a rattling sound it cycled on again as I shut the door. He didn't stir in his bed. I undressed in the dim light from the street, aware of every sound I made. Carefully I edged between the twin beds and climbed into my own.

First I threw off the bedspread. Then the blanket and the sheet. I began to doze, but woke up a few minutes later gasping for breath. The air was as dry as a desert, and it must have been ninety degrees in there. And yet I could see that just across the dark, narrow gulf between beds, Ken was asleep and breathing loudly, huddled under all of his blankets, and a quilt too.

"He's really sick," I murmured to myself, as if explaining to a small child. The dry air made me cough.

I got up and went back out into the family room. Everyone had gone to bed by now, and I must have looked like a ghost dragging my pillow and sheet behind me through the darkened house.

I lay down on the nubby couch, relieved to be by myself, wondering if I had deserted him.

8.

Behind the huge swimming pool rose the bluish, wooded foothills. The lanes went sideways, and stopping to adjust my goggles, I saw arms lifting and falling rhythmically, splashing drops in the sunshine, in rows all down the churning water. I finished my laps and sat down in the sun near Carol's lane.

"Did you have a nice swim?" she asked sweetly, getting out. I shaded my eyes to look at her medium-large form, remembering, when I was very little, how beautiful she seemed to me in her white two-piece bathing suit.

"Really nice," I said. As she dried herself off, I took in her physical imperfections with a glance, comparing the real, older Carol with the glamorous, mysterious figure I had created and loved so much as a child. "Isn't it beautiful here?" I asked.

She looked around at the hills, the tops of live oaks behind the fence.

"It's totally perfect," I said. "I can't believe we found this place."

She sat down next to me on the warm concrete. We didn't have to hurry home. Ken was napping, and dinner wasn't for a few hours.

I told her how glad I was that she was there this week, and that she had said things I wouldn't have been able to say. "It's weird. I totally clam up when I walk into that house," I said.

Carol nodded. "Well, sometimes it's hard to get a word in edgewise." There was the television, and then Mom had taken it upon herself to fill up nearly every other free moment with anecdotes of church or the various trips she and my father had taken since retirement.

"I guess that's her way of dealing with it all," I said, though not generously. But she had been so nice that morning, when she came out to the kitchen and found me sleeping on the couch. "Don't worry," she had said. "If it's too hot in the bedroom, we can set up the Hide-A-Bed for you out here." Suddenly it struck me that she was saying, in essence, "I can't talk to you about Ken's illness, but I can do this for you." I added to Carol, "Otherwise Mom's been awfully sweet."

"And Dad too," she agreed, then appeared to be thinking. I looked up at the very pale sky, blinding myself a moment. "Ken seems kind of out of it, I guess," Carol said. "He sleeps an awful lot."

I told her that he had been very depressed, but left out the part about suicide. I said his health wasn't great.

She shifted on her towel, fingered her calf absently. "He tells you things."

I shrugged. Whatever Ken had to tell me lately only made me feel more and more helpless.

"Do you think you're close because of both of you being gay?"

I had come out to Carol only a month before, and this was the first time we had talked about it face-to-face. Part of me cringed to hear the word that I had left so long unspoken in family settings. I hadn't said anything to my parents yet on the topic. Was it simply that I wasn't ready, or that I couldn't resist the intrigue of coming out to one family member and not others?

"Of course, Ken and I grew up together," I said, meaning that all the other siblings were so much older. "So we're close because of that. But I guess our both being gay has made us closer. And we were out only to each other for so many years."

"I knew Ken was gay," she corrected. "And Janet did too."

I secretly frowned at this intrusion on my sense of holding utterly privileged information. "Oh, that's right . . . "

Shortly a breeze came up, and we gathered our things. We continued the conversation on the way home in the car.

"When you told me you were gay," she said, as I drove past the new public library, "it kind of threw me. It made me question my own sexuality."

I said I could understand that—though I was a little miffed to hear that Carol's acceptance of me was a process rather than a simple fact. A parking lot of cars went by.

"For some reason when Ken came out to me—that must have been something like five years ago—I didn't really think about it much," she went on. "But then two—I guess that made me stop and think."

This was one of my reasons for not coming out to my parents. Maybe they had accepted one gay son, but what if they couldn't accept two? "Huh. And?"

"Well, just that I had to think about it, and about myself. That's all."

I averted my eyes from the broad, tanned shoulders of a teenager in a tank top selling buckets of flowers on the corner. The light changed, and I made a sweeping left turn onto the expressway. "That's interesting," I said.

The grainy pavement wound along an evergreen park. For a moment, we were the only car on the road. Carol asked me about my new boyfriend, Glenn, which made me happy again. "I can't believe I actually met someone I like," I said. I pictured his face in my mind—this secret bright spot in my life, something I was desperate to talk about and that had come to seem unreal over the past few days. Something that was mine.

"I told you Glenn is black," I said, evoking the backdrop of my parents' bigotry, something Carol and I had often discussed. "I think Mom and Dad would have a harder time with that than with my being gay. Especially Dad."

It was almost a relief to be discussing a huge, insoluble problem other than my brother's illness.

"Yeah," Carol agreed. "I was kind of surprised at how accepting they were of Ken after he . . . "

Ahead, a group of cars schooled and slowed in the haze beneath a stoplight. I exited the expressway.

"He's really depressed?" Carol asked.

I frowned, returning to the matter at hand. "It makes him pretty hard to communicate with sometimes."

"It really is," she murmured. "He doesn't really say much." I turned onto our street. "I don't know what to ask him, what to say," Carol burst out. "I don't know what he needs. I just don't know what to do."

I sighed in agreement, and we were silent as I pulled into the drive. I shut off the engine, and Carol thanked me warmly for doing the driving. But I only shrugged, since there was nothing I wanted more at that moment than to be at the wheel.

9.

My mother came in as I was packing. Ken and I were leaving in an hour for San Diego, and already he had taken his bag out to the family room. The weekend was over, and my mother looked very sad.

"I'm sorry I have to go so soon," I said.

She patted the fringe of the rug with her toe. She seemed to have let go of her chattiness for a moment. "All our children live too far away," she sighed.

I went and hugged her. "I know," I said. This was the kind of gesture I couldn't really muster before Ken got sick, before it was so clear how temporary everything is.

I released her, and her guard went up again. "But we did it to our parents," she said, "so I guess we can't complain."

IN THE AIR, Ken dozing next to me, I opened V. S. Naipaul. *And it is as though because you are frightened of something it is bound to come, as though because you are carrying danger with you danger is bound to come. And again it is like a dream. . . .*

The stewardess called to my brother softly from the drink cart, "Sir, sir?" But he was sound asleep, his mouth slack, breathing troubled. I half smiled at the stewardess, embarrassed by illness, by the way the ordinary had been drained out of every such ordinary moment. Nervously I put down my tray table, thanked the stewardess profusely for my orange juice.

In San Diego the planes come in steeply for landings, down a hillside. Out the window, in that brief, suspended moment: the city and then the sea in sunset, spread out before the huge, heavy, lumbering aircraft. We bounced on the runway, and Ken woke with a start, looked around distractedly. The plane began to whoosh and shudder.

"We're here," I cried idiotically. "Are you tired?" He said his stomach was upset. "You'll be home soon," I reassured him.

With excruciating slowness, the aircraft taxied through the arid, flat airfield.

Ken's new sponsor from Narcotics Anonymous would be picking us up. "I'm looking forward to meeting Phil," I said, hoping to make up for years of scarcely visiting Ken in his own city, never meeting any of his friends, never seeing anything about his life until he got sick. "He's a good friend, right?"

My brother nodded vaguely.

"KEN, THERE WAS A LOT of energy, a lot of really good energy there," Phil was saying. We were speeding in his little pickup truck out of the terminal. "I wish you could have been there today!" Apparently there had been some kind of NA conference over the weekend.

"Uh-huh," Ken murmured. He sat hunched like a child between Phil and me in the cab's front seat.

"There were people from all over the country, and the speakers were just really great—weren't they, Deb?"

"Yeah!" Deb was sitting in the camper shell in back, behind the seat.

"There was this one guy, Ken, I wish you could have heard him!"

"Oh, really?" Ken murmured.

There was a fake and excitable quality in Phil's voice that I hadn't heard since Christian meetings back in high school. I stared ahead into the dusk. Perhaps to avoid traffic, Phil took surface streets instead of the freeway, passing through the neighborhoods of San Diego one by one. Each was announced by a huge neon sign stretching across the road in an arch— ornate, pink and blue and orange, perhaps from the fifties.

Phil continued: "He told these amazing stories. He was talking about how he loved doing drugs so much, he got so he'd go for any kind of intensity—any kind. This guy was intense, Ken. He'd do anything! Speed, heroin, PCP, fucking horse tranquilizers." Phil was getting more and more excited. He peered over the steering wheel fervently as he talked, a dark walrus mustache drooping over his mouth. "So one day he gets really high on coke, and he does everything he has, and he searches everywhere in the house for more, and all he can find is a couple 'ludes. He can't find anything else! So he swallows the 'ludes, and he sits down and he says to himself, 'Man, I'm so fucked up, my life is so bad, I'm gonna kill myself.' "

I flinched, glancing at Ken next to me. Phil had paused for dramatic effect, and then he signaled and abruptly changed lanes. I couldn't understand how this kind of talk could possibly help anyone, and I was getting mad. I thought, My brother has AIDS, for God's sake! Even now I can't imagine what compelled Phil to tell the story.

Ken steadied himself with one hand on the dash. And yet his expression was no more or less troubled than before, and whether he was listening closely to Phil or only patiently enduring him, I couldn't tell.

"So, Ken, he starts looking for a knife or something," Phil said. "And this is going to sound really gross, but this guy was so inspiring that it wasn't." I stared at my fingers under the sweeping light of the street lamps. "He goes through all the drawers but he can't find a knife anywhere, so he takes a fork—a fork—and he starts stabbing at the veins in his wrist."

"Phil—" Deb meekly warned.

But Phil spoke with the urgency of an apostle. "So he's stabbing and stabbing, and Ken, he said he couldn't even feel it, he was so high, and he just wanted to feel something, anything—" When would the story end? Was there some way to

rescue Ken from these crazy people? "—and he couldn't punc-
ture the vein, so then he started *pulling the veins out of his wrist
with the fork—*"

Just then I looked up and saw the archway announcing the
next neighborhood, which happened to be our destination:
"Normal Heights," in brilliant pink neon against the twilight.

10.

I woke in a cold sweat in the middle of the night. I shifted on
the couch, which was just barely long enough for me to stretch
out on. I pulled my moist T-shirt away from my chest.

Night sweats. In San Jose, I recalled, I had borrowed Ken's
acne medicine. I used the same applicator he had put directly on
his face. What if it was somehow contaminated with HIV and I
had infected myself? How could I be so stupid? With one care-
less act I'd ruined my life.

AT THE ORGANIC market, the next morning, I caught the eye of
a slender, bearded, bespectacled organic grocery man. I sneezed
in the next aisle. "Bless you," he said. Pushing my cart past, I
considered the man's fine, bare legs.

"Cliff?" Ken called from the dairy case. "Where are you?"

KEN WAS OUT at the doctor's. I shut both doors of the bathroom, lay down on the floor, and masturbated.

IN THE AFTERNOON, we went to his gym. After my swim, more than the usual number of furtive glances in the locker room. A man with a perfect body that somehow belied his hippie beard made a big impression. Then, as I made my way from the shower, I caught sight of Ken's naked body, which somehow appeared both flabby and emaciated, and his familiar, reddish skin. Nervously he held the towel to cover himself as he passed, nodding quickly. "I'll be out in a minute," he said, mustering his familiar older-brother voice of authority and camaraderie.

11.

The freeways in San Diego seemed even newer, more spectacular, and more arid than those in San Jose. They traversed canyons on great, clean, spindly stilts, curving and looping around each other too high in the air. We sped along to the bed store.

"I have to give the deposition next week," he said. Air through his hair in the sunshine. "I knew this would come back to haunt me."

He had been in a car accident in Hawaii three years before. Ken was driving, and he and his boyfriend at the time were having an argument; the accident was Ken's fault. The ex-boyfriend said he had had residual neck and back pain, and now he was suing—not Ken, but the rental-car company. Though Ken had worried about this during several phone conversations before, it was complicated and I still didn't really understand. Something to do with Hawaii's no-fault insurance laws.

"It also brings back that time," Ken said. He had joined Al-Anon because of that boyfriend. This was what later led to Ken's deciding that he himself was addicted to marijuana. "That relationship was really fucked up. I just don't want to think about it, or see him, or his stupid dyke lawyer either."

I tried to unknit my brow. "I could see that." And suddenly I really could, my empathy operating at last, as if some loose connection in the wiring had slipped into place. He was sick, and now, the return of phantoms. I thought of my own ex-boyfriend, also alcoholic, and how much I hated running into him. "So you have to testify in court?"

"Not *testify*," he cried. "Give a *deposition*."

The connection sputtered again, and I swallowed hard, re-verting quickly to about age ten. Ken had always been expert at making me, six years his junior, feel like a complete idiot. "What exactly is a deposition?"

He sighed through his nose. "I have to give a statement to the lawyers." He stared ahead at the bright freeway. Maps along the dash reflected distractingly in the hazy windshield.

"But he's not suing you."

"Cliffy, isn't that what I just said?"

Tears nearly burst at the corners of my eyes, like a cartoon character. I looked out the window, scraggly canyons going past. Another freeway crossed overhead, the approaches twisting and soaring.

"Don't get so defensive," I said at last, my voice shaking. I had been wanting to say something like this for a while now. "I'm just trying to understand."

"You're not listening."

How true this was, I couldn't tell. "I am. Can't I ask a question?"

The highway ticked by. He sighed loudly and suddenly seemed in great emotional pain and regret. He said he was sorry. "I'm really on edge," he said. "I feel like such a bitch."

He changed lanes, the tires thumping smartly over the little bumps. Gazing out the window, I felt as though I had pointed out to him one more great failing, one more sign of his slow decay in the face of illness.

12.

It was during this period, the last six months of Ken's life, that I became obsessive about swimming. It seemed to be the only thing that kept me from losing my mind. And I would descend into an outraged panic if, because of circumstances beyond my control, I wasn't able to get my body into the water at least every other day.

In San Jose, my sister and I had gone to our pool up in the hills nearly every afternoon. In San Diego, kneeling on Ken's living-room floor before the telephone book, I searched for community centers and YMCAs. I called out the names to Ken, who was in the dining room eating breakfast.

"That one's not *too* far," he said. We had gone to his gym the day before, but that had used up his one guest pass. Now I had decided that one swim in two days was not enough, and I had to find another pool.

"Is it open?" I called.

He didn't answer. I went into the dining room, where he sat at the small, informal table that had once been in the family breakfast nook, when we had a breakfast nook, that is, back in Louisiana. For years it had waited up in the garage in San Jose, until Ken took it. I stroked the blond wood, which had escaped my grandfather's varnish and stain. "You got all the good stuff, because you ended up in California."

Ken was earnestly chewing his milky cereal, all meals suddenly full of meaning as he tried to keep his weight up. "Hmm? Oh, yeah. This table really fits perfectly in here."

I sat down, happy to be on the same wavelength for a moment. The room was cool and full of light. "If the pool's open, maybe I could go swim while you go to your dentist's appointment this morning?"

A frown flickered on his face, and his eyes grew almost imperceptibly dull. "All right."

I looked down, feeling caught. I would have imagined myself accompanying Ken to one doctor after another, "really being there for him," helping him through each fearful and unsure step of his terrible disease. But it was barely two days into my visit, and I wanted to get away. In some interior theater a confused, stormy shipwreck scene was playing loudly in black and white: "Save yourself! Jump! Into the lifeboat! Now!"

I said, "You don't mind dropping me off, do you?"

TWELVE LENGTHS warm-up, alternating breast stroke and crawl. Twelve crawl, fast. Six cool-down, alternating breast and crawl. Six kickboard. Four cool-down, breast and crawl. One thousand yards, a number that had somehow come to mean that I must be healthy.

The water was bright turquoise, the reflections blinding. As I rested, the guard tried to impress little girls with judgments. "That's not how you do a flip turn," he said in the nasal and strangely effeminate tones of a California athlete. "Not such a big splash." When the erring swimmer stopped for a moment, the shivering girls stomped the wet patio, pointing. "You're doing it wrong! He said you're doing it wrong!"

I SAT in the sunshine in front of the community center, on the warm, nubby curb. I ran my hand through my wet hair, closing my eyes, calmed in all my soaked, chlorinated limbs. Shortly Ken's dark blue car pulled up before me, somehow faceless in the sun, like a black limo. I got in, and there he was in his sunglasses, his jaw set. He scarcely glanced my way. Was he mad that he had to pick me up? Was this complication too much for one day?

"So? How was the dentist?" I was ready once more to be full of eager, sympathetic curiosity.

We pulled into the street. He said he had to get a prescription filled on the way home. He tapped a piece of paper on the dash.

"What did he give you?"

"Antibiotics." Ken spoke the word as if it were, perhaps, *shit*. "Jesus, and I just got off them. Some vacation."

I began to wonder how all the medicines might interact. He hadn't been on AZT for some time, but he did go in for weekly

treatments to prevent pneumonia, and there were other things
he took—I wasn't sure what.

"What does your doctor say about it?"

"I didn't call him."

He said this in a strange, quick tone, like a teenager getting
away with something. Once again, I felt I had to take some kind
of stand. Perhaps swimming had made me feel invincible.
"Shouldn't you tell your regular doctor the dentist is giving you
antibiotics?"

"I don't want to."

"Ken—"

"Just—" He half turned to me, then turned to his driving
again, his face set. "Because I don't feel like it, that's why."

WE WENT OUT to dinner at a Mexican restaurant downtown,
saying almost nothing through the meal. "This is really nice," I
tried, looking around once more at the dark wood tables, the
Spanish arches. He nodded, frowning at his huge plate of food,
largely untouched. I had begun to wonder again how I was
going to get through the rest of the visit, guiltily wishing I were
back in New York already. "Any of your friends I could meet?" I
asked. It had been two days, just the two of us. And I wanted to
see who else there was besides Phil and Deb. Last Christmas
there had been time only for family "Is there anyone you'd like
to get together with?"

He pushed a leaf of lettuce with his fork. "Not really," he
muttered.

"What?"

"I said, '*Not really.*' Jesus, I feel like I have to yell."

He had been speaking in a very low voice all day, and all day I had been asking him to repeat himself. "I don't need it louder," I said. "I just need it clearer."

"All right." At least he was trying to be nice. He took a bite, chewed in tiny movements that reminded me of my grandfather.

"How about Jeff?" I asked. He had told me Jeff was his best friend.

"Oh, he's really busy this weekend."

I shrugged, resumed with my green enchilada. As the dinner went on, I began to grow utterly bored, drugged by Ken's immobility. "What should we do tonight?"

He looked up—that distracted, distrustful glance again. "I'm pretty tired. We can just see what's on TV."

I said to myself, "He's not feeling well, for Christ's sake." But I wanted this visit to be like old times. And the truth is, I wanted my brother to be a brave poster-child sort of AIDS patient, cheerful and bright eyed to the end, full of life and inspiration despite all he faced. I imagined him founding a support group called Exceptional AIDS Patients. Why wasn't he a hero, a miracle of willpower or recovery, a special case?

Sad and silent, driving home through his neighborhood in dreamy California night, the pebbly whoosh of tires, flat and winding lanes, the curbs white and square in the dim streetlight, quiet yellow-lit windows above lawns, the air moist and cool. When the car stopped, everything was utterly quiet, except for the airy rumble of the distant freeway and a slight, balmy breeze.

The smell of flowers and eucalyptus on the wind seemed almost audible.

We sat in his tiny living room watching television in the dark. I stared, mesmerized as a cat by the checkered, shifting, almost blinding colors. In the middle of the movie, Ken stood up mechanically and, without a word, went into his room and shut the door. It took me several minutes to realize he had gone to bed, not even thinking to say good night.

I lay back on the couch, fingering the drapes. The TV continued on, speaking to the darkened, empty room. No matter what was said between Ken and me, somehow nothing got to the point. I seemed more and more to be dealing only with phantoms—half-formed thoughts, hidden expectations, stand-ins for strong emotions. I dug my journal out of my bag, uncapped my pen, tried to think. What would I want to tell him, if I could say anything?

"I feel like I'm losing you prematurely, to your bad outlook," I wrote.

It seemed then that all my life I had missed him. We fought often when we were young. We played a lot together later in childhood, it's true. But then he went away to college, and after that he moved away with his girlfriend. Even later, after he moved back to California and came out, he was distant, almost always tired and restless at my parents' house.

And yet the problem now wasn't just his being depressed, I had to admit. Lately even his happy moments frightened me. I had begun to notice that I would turn away if he told a joke. I couldn't let go and laugh with him. Immediately I would see the end of it all, and I would feel sad. So I turned away.

13.

Reading through my journals from this time, five years later, I come upon remarkable gaps in the narrative. My brother and I will have a disagreement, and then there will be no follow-up entry, no outcome. Or there will be a glancing reference to some crucial incident from weeks before, but quickly paging back I find nothing about the incident itself. All the key pieces of what happened between my brother and me just aren't there. It leaves me as mystified and as frustrated now as I must have been back then.

My own frailties come back to me too clearly. Here they are, as I read my journals, as I assemble this chronicle of that time: the inept moments I couldn't forgive myself for after he died. It seems I have flown in the face of all practicality by trying to go back and look closely at what happened. Generally one simply ignores one's failings: it's the easiest thing to do and, usually, the most sensible. What I've discovered is that as the years passed I may have forgotten, but I didn't forgive.

Now, the burden of it makes me sad in the evening, irritable at parties. I have to ask of myself a measure of generosity that I just don't have. I've begun once more to wonder: Is there, as they say in Twelve Step land, a higher power to appeal to? One Sunday afternoon, immersed in these questions, I went to see *Raging Bull* and understood a sublime and almost godlike generosity in the camera's simply watching as Jake LaMotta hurts nearly everyone around him and ruins his life. The movie doesn't flinch, nor does it worry that we won't like the fighter if he's too mean, or too brutal, or too deluded. The camera's eye ignores, forgets nothing. And yet we still love him. Another futile blow, another reckless encounter. In this way, I thought to myself, relishing the theater's cavernous darkness, perhaps the movie redefines the heroic. I blinked back tears, readied myself for the closing moment, whatever it might be.

14.

SEPT. 11, 1988

[NEW YORK]

Still feeling out of sorts. With respect to Ken, like I don't want to begin my life in earnest; that it would be callous and dishonest. Sort of like, "Oh well, he's dying and he's suicidal. Back to my novel." Still feeling like I kept my distance and that was the problem. But neither could Carol get near Ken. Maybe no one could.

SEPT. 12

The evening started out really nice. I felt really open, and Glenn and I had a really nice meal. We cooked at his place. A first. All very simple and homey, feeling like I didn't need anything more.

Then we started working on getting his new bed set up, and things changed. I started feeling an edge of irritability on his part. . . .

At some point I asked him if he was feeling invaded. . . . In a moment he said, "Maybe I do feel a little invaded."

SEPT. 13

Maybe it wasn't such a bad thing that I didn't disrupt things in California. Maybe that was the only constructive solution.

SEPT. 15

(. . . this afternoon it hit me again, just feeling lousy and sad, like crying. The uselessness of it all. I've thought about suicide again, not in any serious way, but just as a possible way out. Also as punishment. But mostly by way of giving up.)

SEPT. 17

The weekend begins. I think I really love Glenn.

SEPT. 19

Talked to Ken last night. He was really clammed up. . . .

SEPT. 27

I feel like quitting my job, breaking up with Glenn. Or maybe just plain dying. . . .

OCT. 1

Phone rings and I hear long-distance hiss. But no caller. Ken? Someone trying to get through.

OCT. 30

I had two mice. I was on an airplane. I wasn't supposed to have them, so I hid them under the seat. I found little places for them. I kept taking them out to see if they were all right. I was afraid they would get crushed or they'd escape and I'd have to look for them. But each time they were fine, and I petted them. Except then one turned into an insect as I was putting it back. It kept fluttering its wings so it wouldn't fit anymore in the place I'd found for it.

Later, I was sewing perhaps. A thread broke—and I became hysterical. I fell on the floor sobbing loudly.

NOV. 6

I'm not sure if I need this much sleep or if I'm just being lazy. Many, many hours this weekend.

～

I spoke to Ken yesterday. He sounded good but his health didn't sound so great. Night sweats; low fevers that make him feel disoriented and uncoordinated; forgetfulness; fear of getting really sick again. He was thinking of trying AZT again, of talking to the doctor about it. One study group showed an improvement in T-cell count. Maybe he could tolerate the drug in lower dosage? He gave up on AL-721; it didn't seem to help and it was a big hassle.

～

I just feel a great need of comfort.

NOV. 11

I feel sleepy still. Glands don't hurt. Woke with a pain where chest and throat meet, ready to cough. I don't think I should go out at all today either.

NOV. 15

I fear for my own health. I think, So imagine if you just never got well.

NOV. 22

. . . Ken was saying he didn't understand certain things; Ken described his problems as "esoteric.". . .

NOV. 23

Bad dreams last night. Something about wanting to be close to my mother. Her face quite vivid. In a San Diego house. Out on the highway, which way was Mexico? The wide ocean—circular, so wide—spinning like a platter as we looped the cloverleaf. You turned just past the nuclear plant to get to Ken's. You could see the wires and power lines.

NOV. 26

Strange dream that temptation was contained in having to go live a piece of someone else's life. You couldn't really control when or where you'd be taken. In that other person's life you found all temptation—which was, I think, simply not to live up to that person's life; no, not simply not to play the role, but not to do your best in that role.

NOV. 30

. . . This morning I stood crying in Glenn's shower.

DEC. 1

. . . I said to my boss, "I have a really rough Christmas coming up. I'm not going to be in great shape when I get back." As I felt my own face droop, the worry pass physically over my forehead, I thought, Gee, it must be true.

DEC. 13

A terrible conversation with Ken last night. I'm getting really frustrated again. . . .

I need to call him soon and clear this up. He was very withdrawn again. This feeling that at any moment he might explode. . . .

DEC. 17

I'm afraid he's gearing up for another really shut-down visit. It's a way of punishing us and himself too. I don't know if I can take it. . . .

DEC. 18

I need to call Ken today. Still not very clear on what I want to say. . . .

15.

"Ken, you call me, and then you just clam up. Or you present these totally insoluble problems, and you seem really unclear about everything, and then if I ask you a question, or I make a suggestion, you just blow up at me. I'm so afraid to say anything, and then—" I was trying to muster all my intellectual and emotional ammunition, in the family tradition of winning any argument. But I started to cry. This was the first time I'd done so in his presence. "I don't know what's the point. I don't know what I'm supposed to do, or what you want, and you won't tell me— and then I'm always afraid you're going to get really sick again, so what's the use—" I broke down completely. He waited while I cried into the telephone. Part of me was relieved to be communicating, at last, something that I had been unable to express all these months. And yet I was horrified to have finally laid this truth on the table—my grief, and, therefore, his death.

"Sorry," I muttered, trying to stop. It was no wonder that I finally lost control right in front of him, since over the past year I would find myself crying just about anywhere, anytime, with almost no warning: watching the news, listening to a song, walking down the street, and a thought would cross my mind . . .

I sniffled and sighed a little longer, trying to focus.

"Are you all right?" Ken asked at last. But his voice was toneless.

"Yeah." I took a breath, tried to ready myself for the conversation to resume.

"OK. I'd better go," he said quickly. "Talk to you soon."

16.

The morning before Christmas, Ken arrived from San Diego exhausted and remote. I did not quite realize that his health had, in fact, turned some further corner. And this, in retrospect, tinged every memory of the visit, our last, with significance and regret. "Do you have the tickets?" he asked groggily, lying down on one of the twin beds. We had at last decided to take our train trip to San Diego. But the way things had been going, I wondered if twelve hours on a train together was such a good idea.

"Amtrak wouldn't let me buy them," I said. "There aren't any reserved seats." Somehow—perhaps in my ambivalence, perhaps because everything was so cloudy during that period— I had taken this to mean that I couldn't buy any kind of ticket in advance. "We have to get them at the station, the day we leave."

As soon as I said this, I suspected the faulty logic. Ken made a worried grunt. "That seems strange . . . "

"It won't be full—no one takes the train in California," I said uneasily.

Carol appeared at the door in her tennis shoes. She rocked back and forth on her toes. "So—hike?"

I sprung to my feet. "Great."

I searched for my shoes, and Carol asked Ken if he wanted to come. Since all the pools were closed for Christmas Eve, she and I were driving up to some trails in the hills for a walk. But Ken said no, he was going to rest. He had been depressed for so long that it was hard to tell how much his fatigue was physical, how much emotional.

Now, from this vantage point, the question seems irrelevant. Across time, I want to go and comfort him.

But in that locked-away moment five years ago, in my old room in San Jose, I had other things on my mind. I was mad at him for hanging up on me a week before.

"OK, we'll be back," I said airily. Carol and I left him lying there on the blue, wrinkled spread, one arm over his eyes.

SHADE OF REDWOODS; a brown, rutted trail of needles and dirt; a creek, the trickle of water seeming to slide thickly between rocks full of moss. Washed out in places, the trail curved along the shallow canyon. I was hoping once again to talk to Carol about Ken, not sure where to start.

This was my oldest place of retreat, from high school days, these trails and creeks up Highway 9. Walking silently beside Carol, I spiraled into a familiar melancholy. Though I used to come here for comfort, I had always found it lonely, disappointing.

"I'm sort of worried about this visit down to San Diego with Ken," I admitted. "We've been fighting a lot."

Carol and I stopped and looked out over the ravine. There might have been patches of bright green grass brought by the winter rain, but here it was too shady, all needles and a little clover.

"What about?" Carol asked.

I shrugged and stepped back onto the trail. "I don't know." And in a way, I really didn't.

"I wish I could have gone down to San Diego too," she said after a while. "But it was just too complicated."

Relieved that someone besides me felt unequal to the situation, I reassured her, saying that she had come all the way from France again. "You can't do everything," I said.

WHEN I WALKED IN, Ken was sitting on the old yellow kitchen stool, watching my mother prepare lunch, as we had done since we were kids. "I called Amtrak," he said, turning. He had a glass of water in his shaky hand. "All the trains to San Diego are booked."

I looked at my mother's back, hunched over sandwiches. I could tell they had been discussing this while I was out. "Booked," she repeated.

"Shit," I said. "Really?"

Ken got up and took his glass to the sink. "You blew it on that." He rinsed the glass. "Let's see if you can get us a rental car."

I blinked. Ken looked very sad and distracted, like a worn-out child, as he carefully placed his glass in the dishwasher. I had let him down, and this was the only way he could express it.

"I guess you need someone to blame," said Carol lightly, trying to smooth things over.

But as if the word *blame* were a signal bell, instantly I became furious. My mother and Ken began discussing car-rental prices between themselves. "The drop-off charge will be expensive," she said, shaking her head. I couldn't speak. The path of fuming silence was well worn to my old room, and I took it.

I lay around the rest of the afternoon, trying to read, avoiding Ken, imagining confrontations. "Why didn't *you* buy the tickets? You're the one who lives in California." Both real and imagined conversations floated around me, swarmed into a paralyzing atmosphere. "If you're disappointed about not taking our trip together, why don't you just say so?"

Later, my mother came into my room. "Did you call for a rental car yet?"

I hardly looked up from my pillow. "Not yet."

She shook her head, smiling wanly like I was a hopeless case. She turned and went back down the hall.

The old rivalries and petty alliances were alive in my head. It was me against my brother and my mother.

I felt a head cold coming on.

AFTER KEN DIED, I often wished I could have found it in myself at that moment to—to what? Either put my feelings aside completely, or blurt them out on the spot so they wouldn't fester. Because it came so near the end, the misunderstanding refuses to sit flat, even now, as simply one incident in a long life. And because our aborted train trip wasn't followed by another, happier chain of events, it appears somehow definitive, final.

At last my father shut off the television and unplugged the tree. I opened the Hide-A-Bed, stacking the worn brown couch pillows neatly on the chairs. Shortly I lay dozing, trying not to look as my mother filled the Christmas stockings for the next morning. "All right, Santa's all done," she announced.

For a long time I couldn't sleep. I swallowed and swallowed, testing my sore throat, thinking maybe I was only imagining it.

I stared into the dim, filmy drapes of the sliding door. Now I had some kind of virus, and I might give it to Ken. On top of everything else, I posed a danger to him.

I woke early at the sound of my mother in the kitchen. I cleared my throat, began to sniffle. She came into the family room in her running suit. Already she had taken her morning walk. "Would you like breakfast? Anything you want."

Maybe she was sorry about the way she had acted yesterday about the train tickets. I reached for a Kleenex under my pillow. "I think I'm getting a cold."

"Do you want some tea for your throat, hon?"

I was surprised. It was my mother's most rare, most sympathetic voice. It made me feel privileged, as I would as a child, and strange, like I was getting all the attention when Ken was the one who was really sick.

She felt my forehead.

"Do I have a fever?"

She shook her head. "I don't think so."

"God, I hardly slept." She murmured comfort, and I looked into the familiar, watery eyes behind thick glasses, her rouged cheeks, now aged, her largish, powdered nose. I glanced down again, earnestly smoothing the wrinkles in the sheet. "Ken was really mean about the train tickets," I said. "Saying I blew it like that. And then it felt like you took his side. . . . But we both blew it, not just me."

My mother stroked my forehead. She said she was sorry. "It doesn't matter. You can call Amtrak again today. You'll get down to San Diego one way or another."

"OK," I murmured, but somehow I wasn't satisfied yet, nor sure what else I wanted.

My mother cleared her throat. "I want you to know," she said, "that you're all important to me. All of you kids."

I was slightly embarrassed to hear so exactly the words that my childish heart had secretly wanted to hear. Somehow she had divined what I couldn't myself express, and it amazes me even now that we had this conversation. The truth is that my mother can't always give me what I want, but sometimes she can. This was such a time. I kissed her on the cheek. "Thanks," I said shyly.

But I couldn't leave it at that. I wanted to strengthen my own alliance with her, against Ken. "He's been this way all fall," I whispered, glancing sideways. I began to repeat the telephone arguments of the past several months. "He calls me at all hours, wanting to talk. But then if I say anything, he snaps at me, or he says, 'I'm sick, I can't deal with it.'"

I sighed angrily, conscious of running on, wondering when the thread of my mother's sympathy would break. I grew more and more agitated, tangled up in the problem I was describing. "I'm doing the best I can!" I cried.

My mother sat down on the hassock next to the fold-out bed. She patted her knees significantly. "He has to stand on his own legs," she said slowly and quietly, almost like a television mother. "You can't do it for him. He has to face it himself."

I continued staring down at the folds in my light blue blanket. Was what she said simple and wise, or just a cliché? It sounded a little too much like my mother's way of blithely ignoring what she didn't want to deal with, of not listening, of too often leaving you to your own devices. I shrugged. "I guess so . . . "

But I was desperate for any kind of advice, and I tried to think how she might be right. After all, she and my father had stayed with Ken and cared for him in San Diego for six weeks last year, after he got out of the hospital. This was a display of unexpected strength, perhaps a kind of strength I myself wouldn't have had. Was it possible she really did understand something about this—what you could give, and what you couldn't, to someone who was suffering before you?

After breakfast, I looked down the long, narrow hallway and saw Ken sitting alone on the twin bed in my room. I gathered courage and went to him.

He had just gotten up and was putting on his sneakers. I leaned against my old desk. "So, are you mad that I didn't get the train tickets?"

Slowly he tied his shoe. "No, why?" He sounded very matter-of-fact.

Was I crazy? I gathered more courage. "It sort of hurt my feelings when you said that I screwed up."

He looked up now, smiling, almost glassy-eyed, and I recognized the shallow cheerfulness he often affected since he got sick. Perhaps he, too, wished he could put his feelings aside. "I was just kidding," he said.

I half closed one eye. "Well, it wasn't such a good joke."

"Oh, I'm sorry." His voice was breezy. "Really, I was only kidding." He smiled again and went out of the room to eat breakfast.

17.

Ken decided that he was too tired to drive down, so once more we flew to San Diego.

I see us sitting next to each other on the plane in our costly last-minute seats, waiting to arrive. Instead of feeling motion and distance, we got into a capsule and waited for an hour or two, and then we were there, as if nothing had happened.

I remember we had also waited a long time in the airport in San Jose. I wondered when the intimacy would begin. But even after my parents left and the family holiday pressures were subsiding, his mood didn't lift. He sat next to me at the gate staring, his forehead tense.

San Diego? I remember one day we went to Balboa Park. A huge bed of pansies, hundreds, all colors, impossibly large petals, their big, bearded faces drinking in the sun. Jugglers nearby, a crowd in a circle; a comic monologue by a unicyclist, some remark at which I said to myself, "Take note of this," but now I don't remember what it was.

Ken couldn't walk far. We made our way toward the arboretum. A ravine. Eucalyptus of every kind. We went down a short flight of worn wooden stairs to the path. Ken stopped, shook his head. "Let's not and say we did." Back up the stairs to the sidewalk, Ken stooping, hands on his knees, trying to catch his breath. I overcame shyness and took his arm.

"You're really out of breath?" I asked.

He nodded. We shuffled along slowly.

"Are you always this way lately?"

"Yeah."

I tried to be understanding. "That must be really frustrating." He didn't answer. Wasn't there anything I could do at this moment? I puzzled over what my mother had said. *He has to face it himself.* Exactly how might that be true? Where did that place me, here and now?

Walking beside him, I tried to make my steps slow and small. I knew he needed to leave, but I was disappointed. I wanted to stay longer in the park.

Back at the car, he had to sit a minute. "I'm OK now," he muttered, putting the key in the ignition, nodding as if he had been asked a question.

He has to stand on his own legs. I waited several minutes for him to start the car, wanting to reach over and turn the key myself.

On the way home he told me he had begun to forget things more and more. He couldn't balance his checkbook. He fell asleep at work all the time. Or he went blank and couldn't remember technical things he'd known for years.

I didn't understand then just how serious this was. The old highway curved between lush embankments. I watched the oleanders waving along the shoulder.

"I'm not doing my job," he said. "I put my head down on my desk and go to sleep." His boss had reprimanded him already for not completing projects. But he had a security clearance, and he was afraid to let his employer know that he had AIDS. He was afraid he'd be fired. "I just feel really trapped."

You can't do it for him.

A dead feeling of not knowing what to say. Once again I was overwhelmed, losing my bearings. Partly I had no idea of what he was going through. And partly I didn't want to know; I didn't want it to be true.

Two days before, in San Jose, after the presents had been opened and we were waiting in the family room for Christmas dinner, Ken lay on the orange throw rug before the fireplace. He said his ankles hurt. A year later, I would read an article in the *Times* on AIDS that mentioned pain in the legs. But back then, the complaint seemed perfectly soluble.

"Here," I said. "I do this certain stretch every morning. I learned it in yoga." I stood by the rug and instructed him. "Take your knee, and pull it to your chest."

He brought his knee up maybe halfway.

"Now, extend the leg straight up. Right to the ceiling."

He raised his leg as much as he could, his knee half bent and trembling, his toes raised maybe two feet off the rug.

"No, straighter," I said, imitating the eager tones of my yoga instructor. "Straighter."

He tried to extend his leg further. "That's all I can do," he said, laughing a little. He let his foot drop and shrugged.

"Really?" I sat down again on the hassock. "Well, you'll loosen up if you keep doing it every day."

THE LAST MORNING was cloudy and cold, the air moist and heavy. It was time for me to go. So much had gone unsaid between us during this visit. Perhaps we connected, and perhaps we didn't. Ken drove me to the airport. At the curb by the gate, as his car idled, I leaned across the seat and hugged him good-bye. He didn't hug me back.

Was he angry with me? Was he just tired, or distracted at that moment? He was sick, and just getting up and driving me to the airport was probably a struggle. . . . Anyway, it was time to go, and I got out of the car, took my suitcase from the back, and waved. His face barely registered an acknowledgment. That was the last time I saw him.

18.

I see the story of losing my brother: it begins with the curled fingers of bumpy roots, continues tangling and intertwining more and more, woody, implacable, and ends twisting into a single, black, burned gnarl of trunk.

I had always hoped for that story to open out in some way— for some sort of unraveling to occur, briefly, before the end. I had expected, as in television or the movies, some final scene of reconciliation and healing.

As it was, we were often at odds, I was angry with him, I felt I had let him down, I was trying to figure out how to resolve any of it, how I might talk to him about our differences—and the next thing I knew, he was in the hospital again. Dementia and long distance made all but the simplest communication impossible. And then he died.

Afterward, I clung to the idea that it could have been different, and hated myself that it wasn't. I saw that last reconciliation
scene as one bright page before the end.

"From what I've seen, and from my own life, it doesn't happen that way," my therapist said recently.

"So, the idea is simply unrealistic?"

She nodded. "But that kind of resolution, or something like
it, can happen after someone dies." I wondered if it had in fact
ever happened to me. "After my mother died," she continued,
"three days later, I dreamed she came to me and said, 'If love
could have saved me, I would have lived.'"

I blinked back tears for several minutes. "That's a really
painful dream," I said.

"But the depression I had been feeling just lifted. I had
turned some corner."

Earlier, we had been speaking of how remorse works. Noelle
had said that, on some level, you think that if you had done x
or y—whatever it is you regret not doing, regardless of what it
is—then you could have prevented the one you love from dying.

I stared ahead a while longer, musing. "I think I had a series
of small turning points after Ken died," I said. "But sometimes,
I turn back."

We laughed. There was a pause. Then I told her my own
most decisive dream, which came about six months after Ken
died.

I was in San Diego the day after the memorial service. Ken
arrived to help me clean out the dead brother's house.

I had been working on the clothes closet in the study. Ken

tried on the dead brother's navy blue suit, and it fit him perfectly. I was so glad! I hugged him and said, "I'm so happy
you're taking Ken's suits. They wouldn't fit me, and I wanted
someone to have them."

I released him from the hug, looked into his eyes, and realized the dream's discrepancy: this is Ken come to help, but Ken
is the one who has died.

I woke up.

It was such a gift to me: to see and touch Ken in my dream.
And he had come to help me.

I remember I cried a long time then. How much I wanted to
see him and touch him again. I hadn't even dreamed about him
since he died, and already now it was summer.

Only he could fit those clothes. There is no other Ken, I
thought. He's irreplaceable. So this was what I had been left to
face. And paradoxically, to keep: his uniqueness. The fact that
he was Ken, and he was my brother.

"Let it go," the pop-psychology voices had been saying for
months in my head. But I saw that morning exactly what to let
go of: his whole life. All that he did and felt when he was alive,
including the things about him I wanted to change, the ways he
disappointed me, the decisions I disagreed with, especially that
last year of his life: they were all his. He was his own soul. Only
he could fit his clothes.

WHEN I HAD FINISHED telling this, Noelle said nothing, and I
stared across the room into the recesses of her telephone table.
"Your not saying anything," I began, "it makes me think . . .

maybe a kind of silence surrounds loss." Even now, I regretted not always granting Ken this silence when he was alive and in pain before me. I always felt there had to be something I could do or say.

"There's nothing one can say," Noelle replied. "A silence does surround it. You don't have to do anything with it, make anything out of it. It will make something of itself."

I was quiet a few minutes longer. The session was nearly over. I straightened, not knowing how to bring this emotional hour to a proper end. "I guess I'm going to go swim," I said, shaking myself. She nodded and closed her book.

The Hurry-Up Song

I COULD HARDLY WAIT for each of Ken's visits from college, to resume our play and the running jokes of childhood. His going and returning was the rule for so long that the more recent finality of his death seemed impossible. He would open his suitcase like a book on his bed, and with unrestrained glee I would expound on my latest discoveries—a faster engine for the racing cars; the weird math teacher who picked his nose all day; and a new, truly awful television show to parody: "It's so bad, Ken, you've got to see it!"

That first fall Ken was away, the trial of junior high began, and my best friend, Chris, turned to me more and more reluctantly in the school yard from his new circle of popular and more normal friends. Afternoons, while my mother was at work, I spent a lot of time in Ken's room, staring at the blank cork bulletin board and playing his little Sylvania stereo, which I had been expressly forbidden to do. Ever so carefully I put everything away each day. I imagined he had memorized elaborately each record jacket's exact position, and I worried he'd find me out because one wasn't pulled out precisely half an inch, or another wasn't stored sideways. His old desk was empty now, except for the stained blue blotter where we used to draw together, and the metal desk lamp with the button you had to hold down to make it go on.

When he returned that Christmas, giggling activity and private jokes were restored as well to that corner of the house. Our other, equally long history of bickering seemed forgotten, and he was full of fun and red-faced energy. I wondered if we were friends at last. He would appear at the door of my room with the dog's leash, asking me to come along to the school yard. He took out the Scrabble board or Monopoly almost every day. And he did watch the really awful TV show—a "light drama" starring Henry Fonda—and our long-standing collaboration continued that night in his room. Once again, nothing phony or ordinary could stand up to the withering, fluorescent glow of Ken's desk lamp.

"LOOK, SHE HAS a salad bowl on top of her head!" Ken crowed, as the alien floated in the spaceship's window swooning. Poor misguided thing, she had fallen in love with Dr. Smith—coward, shirker, traitor, saboteur, all of which we now know equals *fag*—and, mesmerized himself, Dr. Smith steered the ship off course to follow her. It was just one of the many reasons the Robinsons never reached Alpha Centauri, instead wandering from one dismal, monster-laden planet to another.

Lost in Space was the first in our series, page after page in ballpoint pen or colored pencils. A simple extension of making jokes before the television, and only a tentative truce in those earlier years when Ken and I quarreled so frequently. He burst out laughing as he drew, while I leaned over his shoulder making suggestions, hoping the moment wouldn't end. Then he read it aloud in funny voices. "Turn the force field on." "I don't know why we keep this thing. All the aliens just walk right through it." The monster, who looks like a cactus, returns at two for the money the family owes for spaceship repairs. "Hmm. A force field. Oh, well." Zap! Crash.

Barely ten, I was torn between parody and tribute. My own cartoons weren't nearly so intent on making fun. When the program went off the air, I wrote to the network: "You can't just leave them out there in space. You have to make one more show, where they get back to Earth." I knew that a final episode had been made of *The Fugitive*, for example, so there was precedent. But my plea also wandered aimlessly: rereading my letter with Ken's merciless eyes, I was too embarrassed to send it.

THE SPACE FAMILY ROBINSON would all too surely survive any papier-mâché or tinfoil calamity. But would the children survive the family? *The Crabbies*, Ken's comic strip about our own family, ran until I was well into high school. My parents, so calm and harmless seeming since they retired, were often angry when we were growing up. It always frightened me, and I came to believe that the world, and everyone in it, was above all volatile.

My brother was no exception. He swore at me; he hit me. I showed off the bruises on my right arm, hoping for sympathy when my mother got home. Calmer in temperament, I resolved to become the opposite of my irrational family—unflappable I would be, reasonable, above reproach or ridicule on that score.

But Ken was always irritable, ever since I can remember—nervous, prone to sudden outbursts long before he was subjected, in addition, to the fearful rigors of a terminal illness. As a baby he took to wailing through the night, and the doctor said all my mother could do was leave him to cry it out.

A frail pencil line cannot protect, but may distract. A cartoon: in Renaissance art, a preparation for some other, more final work. Our cartoons: what indelible expectations and impulses did they prefigure? Which unfortunate adult scenarios, irresistible forms of unhappiness to come? And what strategies of solace or insight?

CHILDHOOD LEAVES few traces—drawings, a stuffed animal, some toys. Photographs and home movies are usually prejudiced by the official auspices of parents. Traces of what it was like to *be* a child are more precious. Before I was born, Janet had a Brownie and therefore her own narrative of that time, from a child's point of view. One Christmas in her apartment in Baltimore, she took out the stacks of pictures and showed me. The camera angle was low to the ground: the dog's face, a little flowering bush, or my brothers in a wagon—all at child's-eye level.

I have this written record, a hundred cartoons in a box, the view from the back bedroom—Ken and I alone and unattended, taking refuge at one end of the house. No parent ever saw these secret documents. Even the ones that weren't about the family were too subversive, too arcane, or simply too illegible to be shown to my mother or father. Ken and I labored over them solely for each other.

But later in the day, back in the family room or the kitchen, I would be amazed at my brother's ability to move in that world again. Didn't we just declare war on both our parents? Hadn't we just showed them up for what they really were? I was too young to shuttle effortlessly between the two realms, back-bedroom desk and dining-room table. Ken did not always nudge me and smirk. As he talked peaceably to my mother, and especially if he laughed at her jokes, I nursed a sense of betrayal. Languishing on the linoleum sidelines, twisting my legs around each other, I plotted some further and more lonely revenge against them both.

SATURDAY NIGHTS, his first summer back from school, Ken and I watched *An American Family*. The documentary went on for months, after the news. My parents went to bed and we turned off all the lights, against my father's admonition that the contrastingly bright picture would hurt our eyes. As if the screen did burn my retina, I can still see Lance Loud appear in the doorway of the plane from Europe, and waltz simpering down the steps with his shirt tied in a knot at his waist. So, I thought, it could strike at any moment: prancing, oblivious shame like a flu. In the darkened family room Ken and I exclaimed our mirth loudly, as if neither of us had any stake in that awkward ceremony. We had to cover our mouths so as not to wake our parents.

But perhaps we also already understood the absurdity of our individual, secret efforts to conform. Sex was always the most exaggerated of our parodies. "Bee-utiful blue muppet!" cried the yellow ones. Their eyes popped out of their heads. "I'm a girl watcher," Ken made them sing. Later, as I made my way through puberty, they also drooled. Ken, fresh from college and his first girlfriend, eagerly embraced the innovation. Their hands clutched the air ravenously. Some of them were queer.

"Are you Lolita's husband? She wants a divorce," says the lawyer. Ken's yellow-muppet voice would have been high and strained as he read from his ballpoint creation. "Don't feel too bad. Maybe it's for the best."

"I know it's for the best. Now I can see my lover, Mr. Henry, the hairdresser."

IN SCHOOL, teachers accused me of cynicism. I looked up the word, but still I was puzzled. Between Ken and my mother, this was simply how I saw the world—brimming with hypocrisy, with uncharted frailties to expose. Wasn't that simply how things were?

So much older, Ken made me jaded beyond my years. At five I knelt transfixed by the Hercules cartoon, and Ken sneered from the stairs. I tilted my head with new knowledge. The animation was terrible, I realized, and the drawings, and the story. It saddened me a little, but right away I said good-bye to Hercules and his cheap ilk. From then on, I would invent for myself far more sophisticated tastes: Bugs Bunny, *Rocky and Bullwinkle.*

For years Ken stood guard. My record collection, for instance. I bought all my albums with him in mind, and even alone in the family room I played them for him, hoping he'd listen through the wall and approve. After he went away to school, he remained the hidden audience, and only guiltily would I listen to Fleetwood Mac or any other "soft rock." I sat rigidly, trying not to tap my foot. Even today I hesitate to get up and dance by myself in my apartment, fearing some ghostly critic.

I inherited his scorn. With boyfriends, hearing anything even remotely resembling criticism, I may go wild. "What was *that* supposed to mean?" I can hardly bear the most gentle teasing. "Really? My hair is too short?"

But looking through Ken's world-weary eyes also had its rewards. Sarcasm was a whole language, subtle and many faceted, the basis of countless friendships to come. Somewhere in college I passed Ken up, creating myself as too sophisticated for newspaper funnies, television, California car culture, and all other forms of bourgeois consumption. I had learned superiority from him, but I found I had to put it aside when I was with him. "I *like* Fleetwood Mac," he might say. Or, I would have to concede, "I guess it can be fun to have a really nice car." Secretly I was disappointed in him, as if he had failed the strict code he himself had taught me.

KEN'S SENSE OF HUMOR alone survived dementia. Barely lucid, he could still laugh at a joke, even over the phone. Perhaps he only recognized the humorous rhythms of speech, the breaks in syntax. Like when you chuckle at something someone has just said, even when you haven't heard a word. My sister Carol read him the funnies as he lay in bed; I told stories on the phone. He didn't always answer questions, but he almost always laughed. His cackle was the same, fooling me, defying the seriousness of his condition.

Though I cherish the cartoons he once drew, there was one I didn't save. I saw it in his study, after he died, tacked up above his desk. Two stick figures carried some blobs to the trash. I recognized the scene from *Love, Medicine and Miracles*, the chapter that told how to visualize and draw your own impossible cure.

The sketch embarrassed me in its futility. But even its serious purpose didn't prevent whimsy. It seemed torn between joke and prayer. The stick figures wore big, round shoes. They had pointed noses off to one side, and I think one stepped on a foot-operated trash can. I saw the familiar and humorous crudity of Ken's drawing, a visual handwriting I knew well (I can easily identify, just from the figures, which childhood cartoons

Ken drew, and which were mine). The HIV blobs were wiggly and full of ballpoint specks, rudimentary as cheap B-movie aliens. He was laughing at the disease, maybe even at his own predicament—at the idea of leaning over his desk making last-ditch drawings, hoping against hope. I doubt he believed in the technique enough even to set his mind at ease, and I imagine he lost interest quickly, unable to sit still for boring and miraculous meditation.

Ken used to recite a favorite *Rocky and Bullwinkle* episode. Boris and Natasha look down from a high cliff and see moose and squirrel at the bottom. Boris proposes simply jumping off to catch them. "We're cartoon characters. We can do anything," he says. As Natasha watches, he makes a running leap. A falling sound. Crash!

Boris in a heap. Taking the long way down, Natasha arrives at his side.

"I found out what happens when cartoon characters jump off cliffs," Boris says. "It *hurts!*"

KEN OFTEN SPOKE in the language of cartoon characters. Besides our made-up words for dismay, *dih* and *der,* there were other peculiar expressions he alone used. When frustrated (if he was in a good mood and didn't need to swear) he would cry out, "Argh!"—not the inarticulate gasp the word implies, but the word itself. Similarly, "Ugh," pronounced "ugg." When cold, a trilling "Burr." Instead of a true Bronx cheer, "Bleee!"

He also favored, perhaps more than most people, the common nonwords: *ouch, yum, icky, oops.* He spoke them loudly and theatrically, somehow more literally than other people. "Cliff! Yuck!" And more than I ever did, he loved the family's special words: *flo-ho,* my mother's Spanish for something that needed tightening; *urshy,* meaning an unappealing, muddy color or an unpleasant taste; *mooshy* (as opposed to mushy) for something that was too soft: "This pear is all mooshy."

Sometimes he sang *dees* and *doos,* pronouncing the sounds almost like they had meaning. "De-de dee," in a minor key, conveyed danger, as on a bad television show. Or, if we were late and had to get ready, he'd say, "We'd better sing 'The Hurry-Up Song.'" And he'd begin a frantic, wordless version of "Surrey with the Fringe on Top," the same sped-up phrase repeated over and over, as if to distract the minute hand:

Dee deedle-lee deedle-lee deedle-lee-dee . . .

At first laughter confused motion, and I couldn't find my socks in the drawer. But then it worked. It did make you hurry up.

Toward a Portrait
of My Father

Y OU'LL NEED holes put in," he said. My father was giving me a few of his old belts, and his waist was several
inches bigger than mine.

"Yes," I said. "I'll have to take them to a shoemaker, I guess."
But already he had opened the drawer of his desk and produced
a leather punch. He was busy looking for the right hole size.

"When I buy a belt," he explained, "the first thing I do is put
more holes in." He said he didn't see why manufacturers of
belts couldn't put holes a half inch apart instead of an inch, to
allow for more exact adjustment.

Some time before he had given me an old belt that I liked
very much, which he must have bought in New York in the
fifties. A simple brown belt with a pattern of lighter brown boxes
and lines.

So today I had asked him for another one. He had taken me into his study and opened the top drawer of the hutch. Inside there was a series of old candy boxes. He took one out. Each box had two rubber bands, one on each end, red, yellow, or green. He took them off and opened the box. "No," he said methodically. I glimpsed several pairs of old glasses in plastic sandwich bags, with rubber bands wrapped tightly around them. He carefully sealed the box and took out another. He removed the rubber bands and lifted the cover. "Socks?" he said, holding it out to me. There were a dozen or more, the black nylon socks he has always worn, tightly packed and rolled up in little balls with rubber bands around each of them. I shook my head.

He took out the next box and opened it. Full of rubber bands. He closed it again.

At last he took out a box from the rear of the drawer, and inside it were coiled several old belts. The ones in the middle were very tightly wound. "Black or brown?" he asked, taking out the belts, which remained half curled out of their lair. He set them down on his desk, flattening them out with his hand and looking up at me.

I picked two brown ones that were like the one he had given me before. "Do you want a black one too?" he asked, holding up a plain black belt of a more recent vintage. I didn't like it. "Here," he said complacently, pushing it toward me. "May as well take a black one. You might want it." I took it to be polite. It is such a rare occasion for him to give something to me.

As he prepared his hole punch, I looked closely at the two brown belts, admiring the little tan lines and boxes. He picked

up one of them and held it out to me. "OK, try it on and we'll
check the size." I put it around my waist and half closed the
tongue of the buckle onto the bare, unpunched leather. "About
there," I said.

Quickly he grasped the belt at the spot and took it from my
waist. He laid it flat on his desk and, keeping his place with one
hand, took out a ruler and pen, and made several dots exactly a
half inch apart in a line on either side of the spot.

Then he began punching the holes. A perfect, tiny circle of
leather leapt onto his desk each time.

"Hey, that thing really works," I said.

"Of course it works," he replied.

There were six or eight inches of leather beyond the holes I
needed. "I guess we can cut that off," he said, and he took out a
very sharp jackknife from his drawer. He cut the belt—"About
there," he muttered—and then carefully tapered the sides. He
handed me the belt.

I tried it on, threading it through the loops this time, and
I buckled it. "Great!" I said, trying to show my appreciation. I
lifted my arms and dropped them, looking at my waist.

"Now, hurry up and give me that back so I can do the other
two," he said, holding out his hand.

Change

It's late, and I lie down to try to sleep. This was Ken's room
when I was growing up. Though this has been my father's study
for years, still I recognize pieces of furniture that used to be

Ken's. It's been ten months now since he died, and this will be our first Christmas without him.

My sister Carol is staying in my old room, because it has the best bed and her back has been acting up. When I arrived, efforts were made to clear away enough of my father's stuff in here for a foam pad and my open suitcase to fit on the floor. My mother kept grumbling, "All this junk. I've asked him to get rid of it. Look at this mess." She pushed a box aside, and carried an old coffee table into her own study. I looked at the bare floor where my bed would go.

The ends of the foam pad just touch the hutch and Ken's old chest of drawers. Before he was sick, we would stay up talking his first night in, laughing, telling stories. But now, alone, I find myself turning to consider the other man left in the house, my father—as one might turn to a stranger at a party, when each realizes that everyone else has, for some reason, left the room.

Surviving

"I cheated death twice," my father likes to say.

One time was when a truck rolled over onto his convertible. I was four and didn't understand the circumstances. I imagined the truck deciding like a huge dog to lie down on the highway just as my father was passing.

My mother says she received a call from the hospital, but no explanation. In terror she drove the seventy-five miles to where my father had been taken. Fortunately he was not badly hurt:

somehow he had found a niche in the crushed car. If the truck had fallen differently, he surely would have been killed.

When he got home from the hospital, I remember my father wearing white tape around his ribs. The red and white convertible was totaled, and he always bought sedans after that.

The other time was when he fell into the East River in winter. This was before I was born. He was inspecting a pier to see if it was sound. "It wasn't," he says. In his wool overcoat and wing tips he dropped through the rotted boards into the icy water. As it turned out, a boat was passing just then—I imagine a tugboat, like the red and white one I use to play with in the bath—and the men threw him a line and pulled him in.

They had to get him out of his wet clothes, so they loaned him some things they had on the boat. The pants and the coat were too big for him, and he had no socks. Back in the city, he had to go to a one-hour optical store for glasses. "By the time I got back to the hotel, I was so hungry I just went straight to the hotel restaurant and ordered dinner," he says. "I sat down there with my coat and pants dragging on the ground, and no socks and an old flannel shirt, and no one said a word." He begins to laugh. "It was New York. No one even noticed."

Stories

I go into his study to look for a book. Reader's Digest condensed volumes, dozens of them, fat and jacketed, line the top shelf. This morning my father held up the one he was reading.

"Four books in one. Condensed," he explained. "And they're all good stories." He called out to my mother in the kitchen. "How many of these do we get a year, Ruth?"

"Four," came the reply.

"Four," he said. "Mom gets them. Of course there are a lot of them around I haven't read yet." I can remember them arriving when I was a child, the sense of anticipation, my mother opening the brown cardboard box like a gift. "When I finish one," he continued, "I put a check mark on the cover." He gestured, pretending to checkmark the book in his hand. "Then, say if I pick it up off the shelf again, I know I've read it. There are lots of them on the shelf with check marks on them." He said, however, that he reads slowly, more slowly than my mother.

"But he remembers everything," my mother said, almost sourly. She had just come in from the kitchen with her crackers.

"Yes, I read slowly, but I remember stories very well," agreed my father.

"I never remember what I read," I said.

"Like this one I read last week," he went on. "The story is very similar to another one I read. Well, or unless I read it before and forgot to check it off . . . "

At His Desk

Every morning he takes out the TV guide, a ruler, ballpoint pen, and yellow highlighter marker, and he draws boxes around the shows he wants to watch that day. Then he highlights the boxes for the shows he especially wants to see.

Sometimes my mother will ask to look at the guide. "What are we watching tonight?" she asks, sardonically, knowing she has no choice.

Secrets

Once I passed his door and saw him, seated at the old library table, blacking out portions of a document with a thick, black Magic Marker.

"What are you doing?" I asked.

"I'm cleaning out my files," he said busily, not looking up. "This is a report I did for the military. It's classified." And he continued reading and paging through, blacking out paragraphs. He planned to throw the file away later that afternoon, he explained. Now it would be safe in the trash.

On another visit he showed me a report on aircraft carriers that he had done during the Vietnam War. It was on how the navy could speed weapons transport on the huge ships, which are actually like floating factories, with warehouses and forklifts, and freight elevators to the guns above. One of my father's solutions was to shrink-wrap bombs onto their wooden pallets with plastic, rather than fasten them down with metal straps, as had formerly been done. The straps were cumbersome, my father explained, and had to be thrown overboard, where sometimes they got caught in the engines.

Photos in the report showed a young woman in Capri pants placing the sheet of clear plastic over the pallet of conical bombs, and then standing beside the finished, shrink-wrapped pallet; in between, some kind of heat had been applied to the plastic. My father explained that the other half of the bombs was stored elsewhere, so that heat would not set them off. It was only when the two halves were assembled later, at the gunnery site, that they made a bomb. "The navy was very happy with the job I did," he said. "I wrote a good report, and I did it on budget." Then he showed me a letter of thanks from the commanding officer on the project.

"Did you go to Vietnam?" I asked, wondering if I had forgotten his taking such a remarkable trip.

"No," he said. "I was called away on another job, and my partner on the navy project had to go."

A little disappointed, I looked down at the letter from the navy. *Your work has helped enormously our efforts in the Tonkin Gulf....*

Rest

Last Christmas, my brother's last visit home before he died, at the airport, my father had encouraging words. "You're just tired. I get tired all the time," he said. "I take a nap every day, and I'm fine. You just need rest."

Ken took his suitcase from my father and placed it carefully on the curb. They shook hands good-bye. "Now, you're going to be fine. Just take care of yourself," my father said. "You're going to live to be seventy-five years old."

And it was funny, because at the time, my father was himself seventy-five years old.

Disgraced (Dream)

My father was a general in the military. I watched him laying out his uniform on his bed. "Now that I'm joining the navy," he said, "they say I have to take off these bars from the air force." And he removed two of the rows of bars.

"Actually," he confided, "I've been stripped of them. It's because I gave myself two rows when actually I was only awarded one. But I thought two looked much better."

I looked closely at the stripped decorations lying on the bed. They were not actually bars, but little green plastic Monopoly houses. Each was a different shape: a big house, a tent, a barracks. They signified all the places the Commander had lived.

Then I saw that my father was crying. I wasn't sure why. Was it that he had lied about his decorations and been disgraced, or that he missed having so many rows of decorations on his uniform?

And why had he told me the truth? I wondered. It was unlikely I'd ever have found out the real reason he gave up his air force bars. I supposed he must have feared I'd discover it after his death, amongst the papers in his room.

A Tree

The day before Christmas. This morning we decided to go see the tree just planted in Ken's honor by family friends, the parents of his best friend in high school. He had kept in touch with them all those years, visiting them each Christmas, and they wanted to remember him.

I thought of asking if we too might plant something for Ken, a lemon tree perhaps, because he had had one in his backyard in San Diego. But then I remembered: my father always complained about having to care for whatever trees we did have in the yard, and he never replaced the ones that died—the Monterey pine and the two apricot trees in back, the olive tree out front, all of which had first sprouted brown mushrooms at the roots and then withered away. "You have to mow around them, and prune them, and they drop fruit and leaves and needles all over the place," my father used to say. "Then they kick the bucket and you have to pay someone to chop them down. The mower still gets caught on that olive stump out front."

My father hates trees.

So Ken's memorial will have to remain a few blocks away. My mother, my sister Carol, and I put our coats on and go out to the family room. My father sits comfortably in his recliner looking out into the backyard, his hands flat on the two armrests.

"Are you sure you don't want to come with?" Carol asks.

"No, no, I'll stay here," he says, sounding strangely jovial. He hasn't yet spoken of Ken, and if we bring him up he always changes the subject.

He follows us to the front door so he can lock it after we leave. We undo the chain lock and the deadbolt and the doorknob lock, and then the deadbolt on the glass storm door. "Fort Knox," my mother says dryly. We go out on the stoop.

"All right," says my mother, putting on her gloves. "We'll be back."

My father stands in stocking feet behind the storm door. "Now, have a nice walk," he says nervously. If I asked him what was wrong, he would whisper that he didn't want the tree to upset my mother. He raises his index finger. "I order the three of you to have a good time on your walk."

UFOs

Everyone on the plane was asleep. It was perfectly quiet. But my father awoke for some reason and looked out the window.

A huge disc flew overhead, not thirty feet from the plane. He saw it clearly: it was large and round, and it had lights on the bottom. It passed directly over the fuselage and disappeared.

My father turned to look at the other passengers, but they were all still asleep, breathing evenly under their little blue airline blankets. He sighed and looked out the window again.

Later, in Chicago, when the plane had landed, as they prepared to deplane, the pilot and copilot emerged from the cockpit. "They just stood there in the aisle, looking at us," my father told me. "They *never* do that."

I felt a chill. "What do you think it was?" I asked.

"A UFO, of course. Aliens."

I nodded solemnly. I'm sure it was real. Clearly my father isn't one to see things.

"The universe is very big," he said, getting up and shaking out the newspaper. I looked up at him. He seemed to have forgotten what he was about to do. "Maybe the aliens haven't fallen from grace," he mused, "and they come to observe us." Then he went into the kitchen for some ice cream.

Chicago

When my father was little, he lived in downtown Chicago, above his father's furniture store. This was the twenties. Once he looked out his window and saw gangsters shooting at each other down in the street. Then they drove off in fast cars.

The Supernatural

My father believes in ESP and the afterlife, people who almost die and travel upward to meet a white light. Once he showed me a *Reader's Digest* article on such experiences. There was an illustration of an operating room, and a man floating above, looking down on himself dying on the table.

When I was little my father often mentioned the predictions of a particular psychic, Edgar Cayce, and because the psychic's name sounded like *Chase* to me, I always confused the topic with my father's enthusiasm for the family tree. I thought he was bragging about a famous family member who could see the future.

My father himself once had a premonition. It was on a train on his way home to Darien from Grand Central one night. The family lived in Connecticut then. This was in the early fifties, before I was born.

"I had just gotten on the train," he told me, "and a man sat down facing me in the car. There were always four seats facing each other in those days. And I looked at this man, and I said to myself, 'He's going to die.'" My father looked at me. I looked away.

"The train started moving," he continued, "and within thirty seconds he fell over in his seat. Heart attack."

Shrimps

"You're lucky," my father once said to me. "You're not a shrimp."

I am five foot ten, exactly my father's height.

"You'll always do well in the business world," he continued. I was just out of college and looking for a job at the time. "All of us. All of us are tall. There aren't any shrimps in the family."

My oldest brother, Paul, is nearly six five, it's true, but Ken was only about five seven. And my sister Janet barely clears five feet.

My father must have seen the beginnings of argument on my face. "Now Janet is tiny, it's true, but it's never stopped her," he said quickly. "She's always done very well. And Ken, he isn't all that tall, but he *looks* tall. He's husky, and he carries himself well, and he dresses nicely." My father squared his own shoulders. "He doesn't act like a short person, so he doesn't look short."

Houses

When I was little, I thought we were rich. My father said we had the best cars and the best house, and we lived in the best neighborhood in the best city in the country. I myself was born in Darien, Connecticut, and there my sisters had known the Lindberghs' daughters.

My father was very proud of the family name. Shortly after the Civil War, he once explained to me, some Negroes tried to take the name of Chase. "But they didn't get away with it," he said.

In fact, we lived in a small tract home in a suburban town in California. The next house was ten feet away. My father was an engineer, my mother a bookkeeper. Both of them always drove their cars at least ten years. They couldn't afford to send any of us to private colleges, and my mother still saves coupons and rubber bands in the kitchen drawer.

It was only recently, driving through a wealthy neighborhood in Connecticut, that I remembered the illusion. I passed a large, white house with columns and a circular drive, a Cadillac parked out front.

"Oh," I said to my companion, pointing, "that's where I always thought we lived."

Crumbs

"Bobby and his wife are two extremely efficient people," my father says with satisfaction. He is speaking of the Scottish couple at church. He takes another bite of Christmas dinner.

"Bobby has just a slight brogue," my mother puts in. "He's lived in this country for fifteen years now—"

Suddenly my father stands up. "I dropped a piece of potato," he says, shaking out his napkin. He stoops by his chair. "I can't see it." He goes into the kitchen and comes back with a flashlight. He shines the beam into the shadow by his chair. The floor is white and speckled linoleum. "Ah," he says, reaching under the table.

Santa

Christmas in France is on the evening news. "Those are some pretty poor-looking Santa Clauses," says my father. "They look awfully skinny."

My sister, who lives in France, tries to explain. "Santa Claus in France isn't fat, Dad."

"There was a Negro," he says—I think of Glenn, and I'm grateful it's "Negro" and not something worse—"There was a Negro who wanted a job as Santa Claus in some mall in Oakland. And when they turned him down, he sued."

"For five million dollars, or something ridiculous like that," my mother puts in.

"Yes, five million," my father says, shaking his head. "Why couldn't he just face the fact that he wasn't right for the part? Santa Claus is not a Negro."

Vaseline

Over dessert, my father explains how he keeps his hands from getting dry. "I place a little dab of Vaseline on each finger on my right hand." He holds up his fingers. "Then I rub it into the fingers of both hands, like that." He pretends to do so. "I only need a little bit, though. Then my hands aren't ever dry."

At some point, and that point may already have been reached, his changeless eccentricity will be seen as simply a matter of age.

"Clifford," he used to call from the bathroom, his voice sarcastic and high pitched, imitating a matron. "You left the rug untidy." And I would have to come back down the hall and straighten the wrinkles out of the baby blue throw rug.

If I talked back, his face would grow red and desperate with rage. He would yell, storm out to wax the car, and maybe kick the dog. My mother, despite her own complaints, would come into my room later and whisper, "Go out and apologize. See what you've done to him?"

A Bad Fight

It was the weekend of my brother's college graduation. I was sixteen. It was a six-hour drive, and because my father and I didn't get along, I hadn't taken a trip with my parents since junior high.

In the car we fought a battle over the windows. My father does not like the windows open. He prefers air-conditioning.

We had been on the road half an hour. My mother's perfume was strong, and the vinyl of the seats cooked in the sun.

"I'm going to suffocate!" I cried.

He made no reply, nor did my mother. In their clip-on sun-glasses they stared straight ahead at the freeway, the last un-finished houses of San Jose sliding past. In a few minutes I carefully pushed the small lever for the window so that it opened a crack. Perhaps if it was open only a little bit, he wouldn't notice.

I lifted my nose to the crack, to the fresh air. I listened to the slight whistling sound. I fell back down and tried to sleep.

In a few moments I heard the short squeak of the window closing its half inch. My father had a switch of his own, on his own armrest, which operated my window too.

THE MUZAK came on. Violins, trombones, a muted trumpet. It was a tape my father had made of the Muzak station in San Jose. "Can you at least turn it down?" I cried, holding my ears.

"It's not loud," said my father.

I put my head between my parents' two bucket seats. "It's louder in back than it is in front!"

"We don't have to listen to it, Dave," said my mother.

"This music is perfectly fine," said my father.

"Well, turn it off in back," I said, slouching against my win-dow. "There's a knob. The one on the left."

My mother found the knob and turned down the speakers in back.

"You are a pill!" my father said, his voice curling upward.

WE GOT OUT of the car in blinding sunlight.

"Denny's," I mumbled. "Do we have to eat that plastic food?"

"Dad likes it," my mother whispered.

Sighing, I shuffled behind her through the glass door.

"I'd just as soon eat somewhere else," my mother whispered to me. I think my father heard her.

GRADUATION was the next day. In the stadium parking lot, my father opened the trunk of the car. He took several old pillows out, beige and faded brown, pillows that used to go on the couch—round, square, oblong. "Take these," he said.

"Why?" I stepped back.

"So we'll have something to sit on. Those bleachers are hard."

I held my hands out, shaking my head. I knew this was treason, but I was filled with the utmost disgust. "I don't want them," I said. "You carry them."

I saw red blotches begin to form under my father's cheeks, but just then my mother came around the side of the car. "We'd better hurry," she said, closing her purse.

GRADUATION was long and hot, and our seats were very high in the bleachers. "Maybe that's Ken," my mother kept saying. My father and I sat on opposite sides of her, and I wouldn't speak to him.

Back at the motel, I heard water running in my parents' room, and then my father came through the adjoining door to my room.

"Mom's in the shower," he said.

I knew this meant I had no protection now. I turned and pretended to arrange the motel stationery on the desk.

"I haven't wanted to upset her," he said, "so I didn't say anything until now." He spoke in a low voice so my mother wouldn't hear. "You have been an utter pill this entire trip, and I've had enough. I didn't want you to come in the first place, but Mom said you could." His voice rose only slightly. "I wish you had never come."

He went out, not even slamming the door. I almost would have preferred he hit me with his belt.

I lay down on the bed a minute, shaking. Outside the picture window, a grove of eucalyptus trees was swaying in a breeze, long leaves crisscrossing. I didn't want to run away. I wanted to get back to San Jose by myself somehow.

But I also wanted to see Ken, and we were meeting him in an hour. After a while I got up and dressed to go out for dinner. Anyway, I was too scared to hitch to San Jose, and I reasoned I didn't have enough money for the train.

Letting Go

I arrived in San Diego two days after my brother died. My parents had been caring for him in his house there for several

weeks, but he died unexpectedly, months before it was predicted, when they had gone back to San Jose for a breather.

At the service, none of the family had wanted to stand before
the gathering, and we let the minister be the sole speaker. But my
father had written a poem, which the minister read out. It was on
graph paper, printed in my father's hurried block letters. It talked
about bringing Ken into the world and letting Ken go.

Back at the house, a lot of my brother's friends came over,
most of them gay, and I was surprised at how my father accepted them so completely. I wondered if I myself should come
out to my parents sooner rather than later, since my father
probably wouldn't mind. But then there was also Glenn. . . .
Anyway, I knew that telling such facts about myself would make
little sense to him, that these aren't the sorts of things he talks
about.

He sat now in his three-piece suit eating a cookie. I heard
someone ask if the blue Thunderbird in the drive had been
Ken's.

"Yes, and it's almost new," said my father, turning. "Want to
buy it?"

Earlier, the two of us had gone to the supermarket to get re-
freshments for after the service. I couldn't decide what to buy,
so I got the same things I would have chosen for a birthday
party at work: fancy cookies, crackers and cheese, soda. My father went to refill the plastic spring-water bottles.

We met back at the car—the same huge, green Mercury he'd
driven for years. It was a glorious sunny day. He opened the
trunk, and I put the bags in.

"There are so many dumb jerks and crooks in the world," he said, looking around the parking lot. "I don't see why it's the good people like Ken who have to die."

This was a rare window into my father's heart. I was embarrassed, and I felt called upon to say something. "No, it doesn't seem fair."

He sighed and closed the trunk.

Trips

The day after Christmas, my father and I are sitting in the family room. My mother is in her study, practicing her violin. She has an orchestra concert in two weeks. My father is napping in the recliner but suddenly opens one eye and then sits up. I look up from my book.

He takes a hard candy from the dish, pops it in his mouth, stares out the sliding glass door at the orange tree, sucking. I wonder what he's thinking about, and it seems clear then that any picture I might have of him would inevitably be full of holes.

"What was your favorite trip?" I ask, trying once more to make conversation. I'm leaving for New York tomorrow.

"Hmm. I don't know," he says, musing. "I'd have to go look at my list."

He takes me into his study and pulls out a tally of every trip he and my mother have taken since they retired thirteen years ago. They go on a long trip two or three times a year.

I lean over his shoulder, and he runs his clean finger down the page: England ... Tahiti ... Hawaii ... Acapulco ... Australia. It's typed, and there's a date and the name of the tour company by each place.

"So. Which one?" I ask.

He pushes the list away. "I don't know," he says thoughtfully, folding his hands in his lap. "They were all nice trips."

Leaving the Beach

1. The Dog

THE TRAIN began to move, and my friend Megan took out her Spanish comic books. About the same time that things started going badly with her boyfriend, Ramon, Megan decided to teach herself Spanish. Since I had recently broken up with Glenn, Megan and I began seeing a lot of each other. This was in June, about a year and half after my brother died.

She opened the comic book and pointed to a crudely drawn blond woman. "See, Cliff? It's interesting: the blonds are usually the heroines."

"Does that make us heroines too?" I asked.

Megan fluffed out her hair. "I'm a bottle heroine."

Haltingly she began translating aloud, guessing at the words, proceeding with what seemed to me infinite patience. *"I cannot ever marry with you*—she's sending her boyfriend away. Oh, wait, this is the flashback," Megan said, pointing. "I already read this part. This is where she gets raped. *My friend and I went walking in the country. As a trick—a joke—we threw some stones at some men by a*—hmm—*a lake. The men chased us and one caught me . . . "* The girl was shown struggling in the man's arms.

"Always sex and peril," I said. "I like the black lightning bolts around her head."

Ashamed, the girl hid at the house of her friend for several days. After her family found her, they had to hide their—

"something. Sin. Shame. Evil," Megan said. "Something like that."

I looked out the window. The train was completing its turn, passing slowly over the highway in a wide arc. I saw the track we were leaving stretch straight on to the left, out to the wilder regions of Long Island. The train creaked and tossed now, like it had given up.

It was as if we had turned off onto a toy or dream railroad. The big silver train floated along the narrow track, and it seemed like we were going places a train wasn't supposed to go—first squeezing between backyards like a boy on the run, then past burned-out factories and littered industrial lots, and finally across marshes and lagoons, tall grass blowing alongside, and our way grown so spindly and dreamy that it seemed there was no track at all.

The station was just two blocks from the water. Behind a boulevard was a neighborhood of low suburban houses, the newer ones covered in raw wood like country homes. It looked like California, the town where I went to school, or San Diego, the place I didn't reach in time to see Ken before he died.

"It's strange how beach towns all look the same," I said to Megan.

Carol called and said she thought I had better come. "He can barely sit up for a half hour, and he sleeps almost all the time. Sometimes he's more lucid than others. I read him the newspaper this morning, and he seemed to enjoy that. Then Mom said, 'You're tiring him out, let him sleep.'"

"So, is there any news?" I asked, hoping for the refuge of objective, medical facts.

"It's so hard to get any information! We finally talked to the visiting nurse yesterday." Carol began then to speak in the calm but concerned tone of a doctor or a kind policeman. "She said the dementia is intermittent but basically irreversible, and it will only get worse. He'll be completely bedridden soon. . . . They don't know, but he probably has about two months." I was silent. The urgency had crept into her voice again. "I think you should come as soon as you can."

"All right," I said, trying to comprehend. "Yes, that's what it sounds like." So my brother would not recover from this bout. He had recovered once before, a year ago, and he had even gone back to work. But not this time.

I heard Carol respond to something. "Oh, he's up," she said to me. "Hold on. I'll bring the phone in there." I heard her saying, "Ken, it's Cliff on the phone. It's Cliff." Then to me, "Here he is."

There was a rustling and then nothing. "Hi, Ken," I said nervously.

It took a minute for him to respond. "Hello." His greeting was slurred, far away, spoken with great effort. Then a long silence.

"So, Carol was there for your birthday?" I had the feeling that if only I asked the right questions, he would somehow become coherent again. If I said the right thing, his mind would be sparked and he would have a lucid moment. "So, how was your birthday?"

"Fine." Though he spoke in a monotone, he sounded almost defensive, like a five-year-old with an officious stranger.

I cleared my throat. "Well, I'll be visiting you too—sometime this month." I wasn't sure when I was coming, and I didn't want to make promises. But I wasn't even sure he could understand "this month." Today, next week, this month—what did that mean? I wasn't sure I was getting through at all.

"I love you," I said.

I heard him breathing with difficulty, as if I could hear him trying to think.

"Come soon."

That was all he said.

"OK, OK, I will. Yes." I tried to fill the silence. "I love you," I repeated, feeling the same embarrassment I always felt when I said that. There was a rustling, and a staticky sound. "Ken? Ken?"

"Uh-huh . . . "

"Ken, can I talk to Mom now? Can you put Mom on?"

"Uh-huh."

THE SKY was cloudy and the beach wasn't crowded. It was our brilliant idea that summer that you could go to the beach on cloudy days as well as sunny ones. Megan and I settled down and looked out across the sand.

Shortly a young couple prepared to make camp behind us. The man, who was olive skinned and finely muscular, stripped to a small, green and black striped Speedo. He went down to the water, his taut back small and neat at the waist.

"So, are you going to fix me up with anyone?" I asked Megan.

"I don't think I know anyone."

It was only a perfunctory question, and she knew it. Glenn had left me only a few weeks ago, for someone else, and I was still trying to digest this. I had been with him two years, longer than I had been with anyone else. It was no effort to conjure him: medium dark complexion, full jaw. Shorter than me, heavy shoulders, narrow waist. Soft-spoken, a tilt to his head, a very kind manner, but elusive . . .

"Well, at least now if I come out to my parents, I don't have to tell them my boyfriend is black," I said. Megan knew what my parents were like, but she only grunted at this sour joke. I sighed, trying to sleep. In the year and a half since Ken's death, there had often been times when I felt Glenn had let me down, and it seemed I was always begging for his attention. Then, this spring, just as I was beginning to feel better about life, he had started seeing someone else. I knew it wasn't working out between us, but still it seemed like one last thing had been taken away from me.

I opened one eye and looked at Megan. "How's Ramon?"

"Oh, he stood me up again." She waved her hand. "Other wise he's just fine."

"Shit." I tried to make the word sound especially sympathetic.

Megan fell silent, and I let the subject drop. Somehow it was easy for us to be quiet together, and that was one reason I liked so much going to the beach with her. It gave me a lot of time to think.

I decided to take a swim. It was only June, there was no sun, and the water was very cold. Cables with colored floats strung parallel to the blackened jetties kept people away from the rocks. I swam to the far cable and back again, which because of the waves was hard going. I thought, Well, at least I can go to the beach and swim in the ocean. This was life. It was cold, my head and the rest of me was all wet, the waves were pushing me, and I was swimming. It seemed like some kind of compensation.

Back at our blanket, I dried off noisily—"God, Megan, that was great!" I felt like a child telling his mother his adventures. "You should go in, Megan!"

But she would have none of it. "How can you do that, just run right into freezing cold water?" Her eyes were still closed.

"Oh, it's bracing," I replied.

There was a muffled noise, as if the phone had been dropped on pillows, and more rustling and then my mother came on.

"Hello, yes," she said, with strained efficiency.

She and my father had been caring for Ken at his home for the past month. She said they were looking for two nurse's aides to help them. "There's someone coming Tuesday. The county is sending him over." She and my father had found a residence hotel; once the home aides were hired my parents would stay at Ken's only during the day. The hotel was nearby and was not expensive, she explained. "I have to get some rest," she said. "I can't do him any good if I don't sleep!"

I tried to reassure her. "Yes, that's true." Instinctively I knew it was imperative to keep my mother from panicking. "It sounds like that will be much better."

She cleared her throat. "It's just very hard to find someone you feel you can trust. The last one they sent—ugh, gee."

She meant the nurse's aide. "Oh, God," I said. "Yeah." I was speaking automatically, thinking. "But I'm sure you'll find someone soon. Hopefully this next one."

"Hopefully . . . " She sighed and jumped to another idea. "Ken didn't even recognize me this morning. 'Where's Mom?' he kept saying. 'Where's Mom?' I was sitting right next to him."

She was trying not to cry, so her tone of voice was strange, as if she were talking about a rude clerk in a store—as if all of this were some kind of terrible and inconsiderate mistake. I paused a minute, wondering how my next statement would hit. "Mom, Carol says I had better come . . . "

She hesitated, sighing. "Yes, I know." I was surprised at how calm she was. "When were you thinking of getting here?"

I FLOPPED onto my stomach and periodically watched the young couple behind us. I could see the foreshortened bulk of the man's torso, the line of the pelvis curving from the side of the hip and into his Speedo. At first his girlfriend, who wasn't particularly beautiful, lay with her arm over his belly. Then she had one white, doughy leg over his. Then she had both legs over him. Then she was lying almost on top of him, both of them pretending to sleep all the while.

I stood to go swimming again, looked stealthily once more at the pair, and saw the book they had flung on the beach blanket: *Honeymoon Getaways.*

A year before I met Glenn, his mother had died of cancer. I thought he of all people would understand what I was going through over the past year, but instead he seemed only to have reached his saturation point. His brother had helped him a little, but it was mostly Glenn who took care of his mother in the months before she died—bathing her, taking her to the doctor, helping her in and out of bed.

I fled into the cold water, diving into a greenish swell. Would my troubles have been hard on anyone? For more than a year after Ken died I saw only Glenn and one or two other friends. Everything irritated me, and I was always telling Glenn he had said something that hurt my feelings. I walked the streets murmuring, "My brother died, my brother died." Or I'd just miss a train and, waiting there on the empty platform, find myself thinking, "No one loves me."

Glenn stopped looking me in the eye about a month after Ken died. His small, black eyes stared off to the side, his dark, heavy jaw impassive. He just nodded "uh-huh, uh-huh" to everything I said, showing no emotion. "What's the matter?" I would ask. He always said he was tired, that was all, and I sat brooding, trying to figure out what he could mean, as if his few words were some cryptic message from a ghost. Or I might bring up an old topic: "When are you going to take the test?" I had taken mine and it was negative, but Glenn kept putting it off. "I'm just not ready to confront that yet," he would say.

I thought now maybe I could see how Glenn might have wanted to take a break from unpleasant topics, and therefore from me. A day at the beach with Megan was like that, a vacation from bereavement. I almost never spoke of my brother with her. That summer even a neutral sort of happiness seemed so tentative. Ken's death and illness dogged me, and almost anything would bring the awful details to mind. Sometimes at the end of a day, lying in bed, I'd say to myself nervously, "I felt OK today." It was like when you're afraid to say, "I don't have a headache anymore," because then you'll notice that in fact you still do.

As it turned out, the fare to San Diego would be nearly a thousand dollars. "But this is an emergency," I told the airline. "Isn't there anything that can be done?"

"I'm sorry, sir."

I had a credit card, but in my panic I was determined to find a cheaper way to go. I called every airline I could think of, and they all said no. It was like I was fighting the implacability and unfairness of my brother's illness, as if by beating the airline industry I could somehow defeat death—or maybe I thought I could somehow lessen the cost of losing him.

Finally I called a tiny ad in the Village Voice. *The fare was three hundred. The woman said I had to pay by cashier's check, and that the ticket would be issued when the check had cleared.*

I hesitated. "So, OK, and what assurance do I have that my ticket is good and that this is all legitimate?"

"Oh, here it comes," said the voice. "I have been operating this business for ten years, and my clients are all over this city. If you're going to start in on that, let's just forget the whole thing now."

"Well, I just wanted—"

She hung up on me.

THIS BEACH was not our intended destination. Earlier, Megan and I had discovered our tickets were wrong, but the conductor had already punched them.

"Well, I guess it's Long Beach," Megan had said.

"But Long Beach is practically in the city," I cried. We were supposed to go to the state park two hours away. "Come on, let's at least try to exchange them. They sold us the wrong tickets."

We got off at the next station. I spoke to the conductor of the train to the state park, several other conductors on the platform, a woman in the ticket office downstairs, and finally the stationmaster, who had to be paged. All of them refused to exchange our tickets, and we didn't have enough money on us to buy new ones. Each time Megan wanted to give up, but each time I said, "Let's try someone else." Finally we sat down again a half hour later, resigned, on the next train to Long Beach.

Megan looked at me closely. "You're very persistent."

I stared at the dirty beige seat in front of me. "I really had my heart set on going to a real beach today," I said, trying to take this small defeat in stride.

I booked a regular flight and called my mother that evening.

"The ticket is going to be really expensive," I said. Quickly I wished I hadn't said this.

"How much?"

"Nine hundred dollars."

My mother took a breath in. I may as well have said nine million. "Nine hundred?" She began breathing quickly. "No, you can't come. No, no, that's too much! You can't."

"But that was the cheapest fare," I said. "There just isn't anything else."

"No, you can wait. You can wait a few weeks for the advance purchase." Her voice was very strained now. "There's no rush to come out here!"

I didn't know what to say then. Why did I mention the money? I had thought I only wanted her to help pay for the ticket. Perhaps I wanted to express the urgency I was feeling, and money seemed the only way.

"And Paul has been here, too," she went on. My oldest brother had arranged a business trip to San Diego that week. "All these visitors— it's tiring him out!" she cried. "Carol was reading to him half the day and not letting him sleep. He was better last week. He needs rest!" She paused a minute, and then she said it: "And I don't want him to get the idea we think he's going to die."

"SOMETHING doesn't smell right," Megan said.

I stopped drying myself off. I had swum to the far cable and back once more. "It's just seaweed," I said, pointing. "Look, there's old seaweed all around." It was a salty, rotten sort of smell. Ragged, brownish shreds and little gray pieces of driftwood were everywhere.

Megan didn't seem convinced.

I sat down, exhausted from my swim, sniffing the air every few minutes. The beach was not clean, it was true. "I think I swam too far," I said, trying to change the subject.

Just then we saw a parks truck arrive and three men in green overalls get out a little ways down the beach. They took shovels from the back, conferred with one another about the spot, and began to dig.

"What are they doing?" I asked.

We watched as they dug a shallow hole. They put their shovels aside and stooped. In a moment we saw them pull at an animal's leg.

"Jesus," Megan cried, turning away. "It's a dead dog."

We both groaned and lay back on the blanket, shutting our eyes.

"Somebody must have buried their dog on the beach," I said. This was more appealing to me than the idea that it had somehow floated in—from the same water where I had just been swimming. There were a lot of old people living in the high-rises along the boardwalk, I reasoned; I imagined one of them doing it—an old man, at night, burying his old dog that had died. "Well, at least they took care of it now," I cooed, speaking like a television mother. "It's all taken care of, dear."

Megan laughed sleepily. "All gone now."

Later, however, when we were leaving to go have dinner, we saw the whitish paw of the dog sticking out of the nearest trash can.

I hurried past, but Megan stopped, suddenly fascinated. "Ooh, I want to go see," she said.

"Megan . . . " I held my nose dramatically. "Come on!"

She hesitated a moment, but then she shook her head and quickly caught up to me. We reached the boardwalk, and I hurried up the steps.

"No wonder it still smelled bad," I gasped. "Why would they put it there?"

Megan shrugged. "I guess they didn't feel like carrying it away."

2. *A Ranger*

In another beach town, in late July, Megan and I sat waiting for breakfast. The floor was dirty gray, the tables red and chipped. Behind the U-shaped counter were empty shelves with one or two doughnuts, it seemed not because all the others had been bought by eager customers, but because there had never been any to begin with.

Megan's deep-set eyes gazed downward, her cheekbones looking especially pronounced. "Is this place depressing you?" I asked. We had planned to have a big breakfast together before the beach this week, but then we walked all the way through town from the station, and this was all we could find. Even now, on the periphery of my grieving, little things like that could bother me, make me feel doomed. "Should we go?" I asked.

But Megan only laughed. "No, it's fine." We turned together and looked at the video game in the corner, a big black booth with bright decals, the violent game scrolling past the screen, making whizzing noises. "It's charming," she laughed.

The waitress, frazzled and middle-aged, foreign but not a hopeful kind of immigrant, returned to explain that she didn't have enough French toast batter for two. I accepted pancakes instead.

"You're very docile today," Megan said.

As usual I was trying to be cheerful and witty. I made a grotesquely docile expression and looked out the window blandly.

Shortly we began to talk about Glenn and Ramon. Megan had just entered therapy and was full of ideas. "It's like everything I do naturally is wrong," she said. "Everyone I've ever been involved with has been really crazy. I seem to respond to that!" She laughed. "It's like whatever my intuition tells me to do, I should do the opposite."

I sipped my bad coffee a minute. "I know. I feel like that with Glenn—I should have seen it coming all along." I said I'd been thinking about a strange joke he once made. "I can't remember what we were talking about, but at some point he said to me, 'If I were your father, I don't think your childhood would have been much different.'"

Megan chuckled wryly. "And what if he was your mother?"

The food arrived, and I began telling Megan some news I had gotten a few days before, regarding exactly how and when Glenn had hooked up with his new boyfriend—and who else knew before I did. "It turns out this woman we know, Sue, introduced him to that guy," I said, quickly growing agitated. "And she's been sort of bragging about it."

Megan rolled her eyes. "That's really nice."

"I figured out she must have set them up quite a while ago, too—like a month at least before Glenn told me about him." My lonely mind had gone to work on it like a puzzle, and I

couldn't sleep all week. "I'm much calmer today," I lied. "Actually I'd like to hurl large pieces of furniture off rooftops. . . . I
called him Friday to yell at him, but he wasn't home."

Megan sighed in sympathy, poking her French toast. "I
haven't been able to reach mine either," she said. "I'm thinking
of just going over there tonight. Is that stupid?"

I shrugged. Ramon, whom Megan knew from one of her
teaching jobs, had just been fired and was refusing all help and
advice. He had been on probation a long time for canceling too
many classes, and finally the dean let him go. Now he went out
drinking every night and wouldn't answer his phone.

"We can't control them," Megan said, speaking in a particular voice she uses, like a mad professor in a movie.

*When I was twelve, and my grandfather was dying, my mother went
to visit him in Chicago and told him she was there on some sort of
business. This was a trip of more than two thousand miles, by a part-
time bookkeeper in a wig shop, who rarely flew anywhere and had
never traveled before without her husband. Could my grandfather
have believed her? I remember my mother explaining how for him
disease was, above all, a spiritual and mental struggle. My grandfather's outlook was important, she said, so she didn't want him to
think he was dying.*

*"Mom," I said now, "when Carol called . . . " I didn't know how
to calm her down or change her mind about my coming. "Mom, Carol
said—"*

*"Things just aren't that bad," my mother cried. Now that Carol
had left, she seemed to have changed her mind. "There's plenty of*

time. The doctor said it could be six months! He's just very overtired right now."

I didn't know whom to believe. On the one hand, Carol had been quite clear that it was urgent for me to come. On the other, my mother had been staying with Ken for weeks, and she surely knew better than Carol, who had only been visiting, what his condition really was. Anyway, since my mother was the one responsible for his care, I felt I had to respect her wishes. But even now I wonder if I should have trusted my intuition and disobeyed her. "Mom," I persisted, "he said, 'Come soon.' That's what Ken said to me Sunday. 'Come soon.'"

"He's not always coherent," she said quickly. "He could have thought you were in California already, or that you were back in college or something, or around the corner. You just don't know."

"But he said, 'Come soon . . . '"

My mother sighed. "He didn't know what he was saying."

IT WAS INCREDIBLY bright, and hazy. We plodded along the dry, fine, peaked sand until we began to pant. Megan changed course and we switched to the hard, wet surface near the water. "Oh, much better," Megan said. "There's the story that Einstein figured out why that is. He was at the beach one day and it came to him. Surface tension or something."

The tan, wet sand glistened under our feet.

"Here?" Megan asked.

We began unpacking. "I don't think you've adequately complimented me on my new bag," I said, trying to be carefree. I lifted it and set it down again, blue canvas with a big black strap.

It was part of a self-improvement campaign. "I had expected you to be so proud of me." All summer Megan had told me I had to get a new shoulder bag. "Now I'm sure to find a new boyfriend."

"Appearances are important," she said dryly.

I began putting on sunblock, which takes me a very long time. Megan sat patiently, waiting to put it on my back. I smoothed it on my shoulders, my collarbone, my chest. It was gooey and white, and it wouldn't quite rub in. I began on the tops of my legs.

"Jesus, are you ever going to finish?" Megan said at last.

I continued rubbing. "Megan, if I miss even one little spot, it will be bright red." I remembered having the same discussion once the summer before with Glenn, an awful vacation on Cape Cod.

"OK, OK," Megan said.

"No, really, it's happened before. I can't just dab a little here and there like you do. I'll have a spot the color of—" I looked around and saw the red markers down the beach, at the edge of the lifeguard area. "—the color of that flag there."

Having decided not to go immediately, I tried to console myself that my sister had only panicked and there was, as my mother said, no hurry.

In fact, my mother was so sure of Ken's condition that she and my father left San Diego the following week and returned to San Jose. They had been away from home for weeks and there were things that needed to be done. They left Ken in the care of the two home aides and planned to return in two weeks. It was agreed that I would come visit after that.

But after only two days the aides began reporting bad news. Ken was having more difficulty breathing, and he seemed to be in more and more pain. My mother was constantly on the telephone trying to understand what was going on. One of the aides—his name was Clifford—was hard to deal with, my mother told me. He didn't explain things very well, and he didn't seem to listen to my mother's instructions.

I had heard about this Clifford the week before. He could be very patient with Ken, my mother said, but already there had been problems during Clifford's first week. He was qualified to give baths, cook, and do laundry, and that's what he was hired to do, but he nonetheless insisted on lecturing my mother on Ken's condition. "I've worked with AIDS patients many times before," he told her, and in his heedless singsong he'd predict what treatment would next be offered by the doctor, and what effect that treatment would have. He seemed to perceive himself as the one in charge, often telling the other home aide what to do. My mother had had to admonish him not to make decisions but to call her or the visiting nurse for advice.

My mother said Ken didn't seem to like Clifford, and I began to harbor a fear that in his confusion Ken would somehow think that this Clifford was me, finally come to visit. Clifford was like a nightmare version of myself there in San Diego, caring for Ken when I couldn't, bustling around his bed, baby-talking to him in an officious nurse's voice . . .

One night Ken was especially lethargic when it was time to be washed, and Clifford panicked. Without calling anyone, he sent for an ambulance and had Ken taken to the emergency room. My mother was furious. "I told Clifford no hospitals! Over and over, I told him. That's what Ken kept saying when we checked him out last month." She was breathing hard and she spoke with great emphasis, like one defending herself against some unreasonable authority. "He doesn't want to go into the hospital again!"

Ken was taken home, but he was soon put on morphine. He no longer got out of bed at all, and his breathing grew worse. I think my mother didn't want to see this as a crisis, which is why she didn't go back down to San Diego immediately. Now it all seems clear, but at the time, even the doctors didn't understand what these new developments meant—or if they did, no one told us. "I just don't know what to do!" my mother kept saying.

"Do you want me to go to San Diego this weekend?" I asked. By this time I had found a good charter flight. "It's only three hundred," I reassured her. "I could go this weekend."

"What? Oh." I heard her breathing. "You could?"

In fact, I was terrified of going by myself, and I had no idea what I would do when I got there, what I would tell Clifford or anyone else to do. My brother was dying, and I had no idea how to help. "Yes," I said. "I could get a ticket tomorrow."

She sounded a little relieved. "All right, please. That would be a big help." She sighed. "There's only so much I can do from here . . ."

That was Monday. I booked a flight for Friday. On Wednesday my mother called to tell me that Ken had died.

THIS WAS THE BEACH Megan and I had wanted to try back in June. It was further out even than our usual beach since then, more pristine, less crowded, the sand a narrow and steep strip between green dunes and the water. It seemed almost wild, and there were wild roses all along the path to the concession area and the bus stop. Their petals were pink and floppy, and their odor was strong and sweet, like the air everywhere in San Diego the weekend of the memorial service.

Carefully I carried lemonade and hot dogs back to Megan. Just outside the picnic area I spotted one of the other two gay men I had seen earlier on the bus, shaking out his towel repeatedly on a small lawn. I watched his slender, surprisingly appealing body, feeling ridiculous that I was carrying a tray full of hot dogs. He turned, and we looked at one another with a strangely neutral curiosity.

I remembered the first time Glenn and I met, at a Valentine's Day party. He said he was a painter, and I told him about the orange and black cityscape from Woolworth's in my parents' family room. He nodded with twinkling attention, and I suspected that here was someone I could really talk to. We sat in a corner, and I watched his foot wiggle on his knee. He said, "My mother had a still life that was three-dimensional. The bowl and the pieces of fruit were raised, like that was more realistic." He made a cupping gesture with his hand, and I reached down and untied his tennis shoe.

I entered the sandy path with the wild roses and began to argue with him in my head. "How could you be so dishonest? How could you lie to me like that?" He waited weeks to tell me he was seeing someone else. A forgivable crime in itself, but I had also figured out that before he told me, we had had dinner with that woman Sue and two other new friends of ours—Susan and Suzanne were their names. All of them must have known about Glenn's new boyfriend. Over dessert he began running his fingers through my hair as the three of them watched, mesmerized. I had wondered at the time why it was such a strange evening.

He had left me to find out these things months after we had already broken up, when it was too late for me to do anything about it. Our parting had been fairly calm, but now I was absolutely furious. I walked along the beach, my head beginning to hurt in the particular way it had been hurting all week, like a hangover. The lemonade sloshed and spilled. I thought that if I could somehow construct the perfect argument, I would at last be right in Glenn's eyes. I wanted to lay down the law. "You fucking coward. What did you think, that this wouldn't get back to me? Oh yeah, right."

MEGAN AND I stayed into the early evening, until the light began to slant and the water grew velvety and molten. Megan sat alone by the water's edge fingering the sand, slender in her black suit, and I thought Ramon would come around soon if he was smart. I went swimming one last time.

Unfortunately, the buses to the train station stopped running before the beach closed. We sat on the bench watching cars go past for a half hour or more. "They're all laughing at us," I said. "There's no bus coming." But it was getting not to be a joke anymore.

At the park office, a young ranger, tubby and tall with thick glasses, agreed to take us to the station. "You're lucky," he said, opening the door of the squad car. "Anyone else on duty would have made you call a cab."

I had to ride in back, behind the wire screen. Megan sat up front. "This isn't so bad," I said, shutting the door uneasily. I checked the handle and confirmed that it would not open from the inside.

But though I expected claustrophobia, once we got rolling it seemed to me not much different from riding alone in the back of my parents' car, behind their high, tombstone headrests. I joked to myself, "These wire screens could be a new product for parents to keep their children at bay."

We drove in silence for a few minutes toward the causeway, the radio squawking. *"Three white teenagers in a Ford van proceeding on the parkway in the wrong direction. . . . Alcohol involved . . . "* I thought it would be wise to make conversation with the ranger, since he had made it clear he was doing us such a favor. I introduced myself and Megan.

"I'm Chris," he replied gruffly.

"Oh, Chris," I blurted. "That's what people always call me by accident. Cliff, Chris."

In silence we climbed the long bridge in the fast lane. I watched the other cars on the road from the new perspective of the back of a police car.

"Now I know what it's like to be a perpetrator," I offered.

Chris seemed to loosen up then, handing Megan his nightstick. "You can poke at him with this if you want."

I chuckled loudly. I decided it was easier if he thought I was Megan's boyfriend.

"You two from Manhattan?" he asked.

"Brooklyn," Megan said.

Chris explained that he had grown up in Park Slope. "Eighth Avenue and Eighth Street. Four-ninety-nine Eighth Street. You can go look at the building. Four-ninety-nine," he repeated.

"Huh," I said. The radio continued to squawk. "This must be a big change living out here by the ocean."

"Oh, I haven't lived in Brooklyn since I was eight," he replied. "We got out just in time."

As in a conversation with my father, I wondered if some unpleasant commentary on certain racial groups was coming next. Fortunately he fell silent and began fiddling with his radio.

We were just reaching the end of the bridge, and Chris began to accelerate rapidly. Shortly we were speeding along at about eighty-five. "This is great," I said to myself, feeling the movement of the heavy squad car. "I guess when you're a cop, you can go as fast as you want." We would reach the station in no time. Already I was thinking how I'd be home soon and I could try to call Glenn once more. "I can finally get this off my chest," I thought.

But then we were suddenly slowing down again, as if life could never again allow me to get anywhere ahead of time. Chris turned to Megan, lifting one hand from the steering wheel in a kind of shrug, apologetic. "I was starting to pursue someone. But then I remembered you two were in the car with me and I couldn't do that now."

3. The Flies

It was another two weeks before I reached Glenn. As it turned out, he was in Italy with his new boyfriend. This was the trip Glenn had once planned to take with me.

I thought I had cooled down, but as soon as I heard Glenn's voice my hands began to shake. I told him the things I had learned, how he had lied to me, how others knew before I did. I recalled our dinner with the three Sues.

"How could you do that to me, Glenn?" My voice was cracking, and I decided not to hide it.

"I'm sorry. . . . I'm sorry," he sighed. He sounded genuinely upset, a rare thing for him. "I'm sorry about a lot of things."

I sat staring miserably at the phone cord, which for the past two years seemed to be the conduit for every kind of bad news and unhappiness.

"I'm sorry I went away with someone I didn't really care about," Glenn said at last. "I'm sorry I wasn't with you."

I looked sideways, as if this was some kind of trick. Somehow I had never imagined this answer. "Why are you saying that? Why are you telling me this, Glenn?"

"Because it's true." And he began to cry.

MEGAN AND I trudged down the sand, past the slatted wood fences. The sun had come out as soon as we arrived. I looked up, and it seemed it was cloudy everywhere but right here. And though it was a Sunday, and this was the most popular beach, it was not at all crowded.

"Well, something had to go right this summer," Megan said. "I guess this is it."

The sand was firm and well packed from a week of rain. "We were presented with a choice, before we were ever born," I said. "You can have love, or you can go to the beach this summer. We chose the beach."

We had, in fact, gone to the beach almost every weekend this season. Now it was nearly Labor Day. I stared at the peaks of sand below my feet. "Walking through sand. This is exactly what we needed to learn for our next life."

We reached a low, recently flooded area, strangely flat and grayish, wide and full of broken white shells, though the water was another five hundred yards off at least. "Ouch," I cried. The shells cut my feet.

"It's like mud," Megan said. The sand was especially hard-packed here, unpeaked. "I wonder what Einstein would say about this."

The ground rose and grew soft and sandy again. We stood and viewed the ocean from the top of a small rise, below which a shallow trough had been created, two inches of water, and beyond that another strip of dry sand, and then the sea.

"Weird," Megan said. We had never seen it like that here before, and I thought of all the changes the week of hard rain had wrought.

I looked around—the new sun, which seemed to be here to stay, big white clouds retreating, light green grass on the dunes, bright sand, the water. "What an incredible day," I cried, turning, wishing that that were enough.

"Cute guys," Megan said, her tone surprisingly light.

A group of lifeguards was pushing a boat in from the waves.

That was a new thing for Megan to say, I thought, unfurling the beach blanket. She had been too busy all summer fighting with Ramon to point out any lifeguards. Now things were going more smoothly, she had told me. Ramon had decided to go back to school for another degree. He had even come over and fixed her kitchen light this weekend, and then he stayed the night. Maybe things will work out for them, I thought.

Meanwhile, Glenn and I were supposed to have dinner again that week, our second meeting. He had lied to me, it was true, and I didn't want to trust him, but something told me to try again. Maybe I could see things more clearly this time around, I thought. He and I had never even known each other before my brother was sick; it was one of the first things I told him about myself. Already I was grieving, anticipating the end; and then Ken died. For two years that disillusionment permeated and colored everything. But now I was coming out of it.

And then there was his dark, somber face before me in the restaurant—restored to me—his eyes bright and intent behind a new pair of glasses . . .

SHORTLY I woke. "I'm going in!" I cried, and ran down the beach.

The water was light green and full of seaweed, very clean, and cold from the rain. More like June, I thought, not quite shivering. I waded in farther. The waves were little and broke completely where the water was just at your waist. But they turned out to be perfect body-surfing waves, very gentle and very effective. You stood there waiting for them, not minding the shallow water, and, seeing the surface rise, you took your opportunity as always, swam eagerly toward shore, and then they carried you in to just two or three inches of water. I swam for a half hour or more alongside one of the teenage guards, watching his thick back as he paddled around on a small board waiting for the next wave. He called out to me. "Best waves all year!"

"I'M GLAD it's almost fall," Megan said. Around her lay books and newspapers. Her efforts at Spanish had succeeded: by now she had graduated to *El Diario* and *One Hundred Years of Solitude*. "God, Cliff, what an awful summer."

It was true. "Well, even so, I don't want it to end," I said. I was almost disappointed that Glenn and I might get back together, because it meant this particular time was over. In retrospect the season seemed very pure.

"If you have a boyfriend again, you won't have so much time to see me," Megan said.

That was another thing about this summer I didn't want to end—these long days with Megan, time stretching unbounded in the sandy afternoons. "You'll be busy too," I replied, meaning recent developments with Ramon.

"Yeah, well, we'll see." She lay back amid her Spanish books and closed her eyes.

The waves were particularly beautiful to watch today, sparkling at the break and foamy in the shallows. I began to feel sad. The fecund smell of fresh, wet seaweed was especially strong— the way it is in California.

That Christmas in San Diego, the afternoon when Ken and my parents and I walked tentatively along the beach, I took his picture on the rocks. Though he had almost died, it seemed all our hopes for his recovery were working. He was weak, but he laughed easily that weekend—his high, cackling laugh, infectious and feeding itself in waves, always over something recklessly and elaborately imagined, the laugh I learned from him and remember from childhood.

But in the picture I took, Ken looks out from under his wide-brimmed hat doubtfully, his brow furrowed, trying to smile and succeeding only with a few teeth, his face gaunt—the clear winter sky and cold sea behind him.

Later my mother spoke to Ken's social worker. The woman explained that this kind of end was common: the primary caregiver leaves for some reason or another, and the patient simply gives up. It wasn't my mother's fault, the social worker said. If she and my father had stayed, Ken might have gone on for two or three more months—on morphine, bedridden, his mind gone, barely breathing.

I was at work when my mother called. Mechanically I told my boss that my brother had died, and I went about preparing to leave the office. Glenn was working in his studio that day and he didn't have a phone, so I just got in a cab and went there. It was strange to be speed-

*ing down Broadway in the middle of the day, riding in a cab instead of
on the subway, watching buildings go by. I imagine it was a Checker
cab, though of course there were no more Checkers by then. But the
space inside the cab seemed huge and dark, and the ride somehow
timeless.*

*I wasn't even positive I would find Glenn, and I remember the re-
lief I felt when he opened his door. Behind him, the walls were hung
crookedly with half-finished drawings. I told him the news, he held
me, and I began to cry.*

I GOT UP and went for a walk, staring down at the yellowish
shallows, and the sand.

The marked child goes through the day. The orphan brain
sings to itself. Some hear the voice of their loved one, encouraging them. Sometimes I imagined that—but rarely. And neither
did I try to speak to my brother in the middle of the night. Even
now it was too hard to define the shape of what had been lost.
Childhood; and, as an adult, a succession of long-distance phone
calls, occasional visits. My days were ostensibly no different
now; we could simply have neglected to call one another all this
time. He was like money I had left in the bank, and now it was
gone.

I didn't feel my brother had died justly, or for a just cause, or
in a manner having dignity, or that his suffering was of any use
to him or anyone else, or even that he was in any sort of heaven
that I could imagine. I only grew used to it all, and to the fact
that none of the facts could have been changed: they simply

began to take their place in a bigger world, and time filled in on the other side, like sand against a jetty. He was cremated and he has no grave, but I thought maybe the sky or the horizon could somehow know the moment and place of his death (a small house in San Diego, February 22, 1989), or that of my loss (my desk at work, later that day, phone in hand, listening to my mother's shaky voice)—that one small place; for me, a notch in the world.

By now I had walked quite a ways. I turned back down the beach toward Megan and the blanket. In a while I saw her there, sleeping. I had picked up shells for her on my way: a black, round fan, a white one the same shape, and a small, worn lozenge of mother-of-pearl, black around the edges.

I lay back in the sun and sighed. Megan turned her head groggily. "Are you OK?"

I nodded. "I was just thinking." But I asked myself the same question, and listened carefully a moment, as if learning my own language. I didn't seem to need to talk, and just then I couldn't have explained my thoughts anyway. "I'm good," I decided.

Megan closed her eyes again. "All right," she said doubtfully.

I nestled into the hard sand and felt almost serene, and sleepy. In a moment I could hear the thuds of footsteps as people passed nearby.

THE FLIES came in twos and threes at first. We thought that we were simply trapped in a small swarm of them, that they had for some reason picked us out, as gnats will. Soon there were more of them, landing on our legs, our ears, the blanket. They were somewhere between gnats and flies, and they wouldn't be shooed unless you actually pushed them off or killed them.

I watched one land near the blanket and nose into the sand blindly as if expecting food. Next to me, Megan sat slapping the air. The shells I had left her were scattered. Finally I stood up, swatting at my legs.

"Maybe it's the suntan lotion," she said.

"But you aren't even wearing any. Or hardly any at all."

"You didn't put any on either?" I shook my head. I was tan by now, and besides, we had come so late in the day that I didn't need any. "Look," Megan said, pointing.

All down the beach, people were flailing their arms, waving towels in the air.

"It's not just us," I said.

We looked back at the white blanket, where several were crawling now.

"God, get away!" I cried, swatting at them. "They don't fly away," I said.

"They're dying," Megan replied. "Look, they're weak. They can't get up."

More had landed on the blanket, long brownish bodies and gold, transparent wings, crawling listlessly as baby possums toward their milk. "No, they're just wimpy," I said. "You know how gnats can be really wimpy?" I recalled the tiny black gnats in the school yard, how Ken and I used to call them "Leonards"—our generic fall-guy name—because you could simply bat at them right in the air and kill them.

"They came here to die," Megan said.

I pushed one off my arm, and it fell fluttering to the blanket. "This is a fucking plague of Egypt. I'm going swimming until they go away."

"That's right, leave me here."

I ran into the water, dunked myself, swam back and forth a few times. But the waves had gone and it was cold. I came back in.

"Is it any better?" I asked, shaking out my towel.

"No." Megan sat looking at her arms and legs to see if any had landed on her.

"Maybe we should ask the lifeguards," I said. "Maybe they'll know—"

"—if they're going to go away. Yeah," said Megan eagerly, getting up.

We walked down the beach to the high white chair, where one guard sat and two others stood by.

"Hi," I said. "Are these going to go away soon?"

The one in the chair was older, and sat there swatting the air with his towel. He spoke like a scientist. "The wind shifted and blew them here against their will," he said. "They don't want to be here. They have no choice."

"Oh," I said, smiling at the younger guard who stood by, and catching sight then of his perfect chest and abdomen between the half-zipped sweatshirt. I looked away quickly, scanning the buggy air. "So this isn't going to stop?"

"It happens when the wind comes from the north," said the one in the chair. "Unless the wind shifts again, they're here to stay. Hey, you got any bug spray? Because if you do, give it to me, please." By now he had put the towel on his head. He was quite a comedian. "You two can leave. I can't." He batted at the air around his thigh. "You heard of *The Birds*. This is *The Flies*."

I looked at Megan and shrugged.

We walked back to our blanket, the sun in our eyes. "And it was such a perfect day," I said in mock pettishness. We stood for a moment looking down the beach. In fact, by now nearly everyone had left. "I guess if they were going to go away, the guards would have said so."

Megan sighed. We had been here only an hour and a half.

"I guess we should go," I said. But I wasn't really unhappy; somehow the scourge of the flies had taken me out of myself, and I was glad for so small and so tangible a crisis.

We had to empty our bags and shake them, because the bugs had crawled inside, between our clothes and books. At last we were packed up and headed toward the pale brick concession building, which stood in the sunshine like a great sand castle. A few people remained, sitting at the aluminum picnic tables, but they too were swatting their heads miserably, and after Megan and I had put on our shoes we turned down the path to the bus.

The light angled steeply before us, already like September. We saw the bugs clearly then, against the darkness of the trees, thousands upon thousands of them, swarming, lit by the yellow late-afternoon sun.

We would come to the beach just a few more weekends that season. The bus's windshield was covered with specks, and the full load of beach survivors was strangely quiet as we traversed the water's causeway—quiet and relieved and expectant, as if we were a heroic and exiled people, driven by plagues into a new land.